This edition published in 1998 by
Thunder Bay Press
5880 Oberlin Drive, Suite 400
San Diego, California 92121
1-800-284-3580

http://www.admsweb.com

Produced by
PRC Publishing Ltd,
Kiln House, 210 New Kings Road, London SW6 4NZ

ISBN 1 57145 169 2
(or Library of Congress CIP data if available)

1 2 3 4 5 98 99 00 01 02

Printed and bound in Singapore

DOGS

A Guide to Popular Breeds

WILLIAM MOORES
& PADDY CUTTS

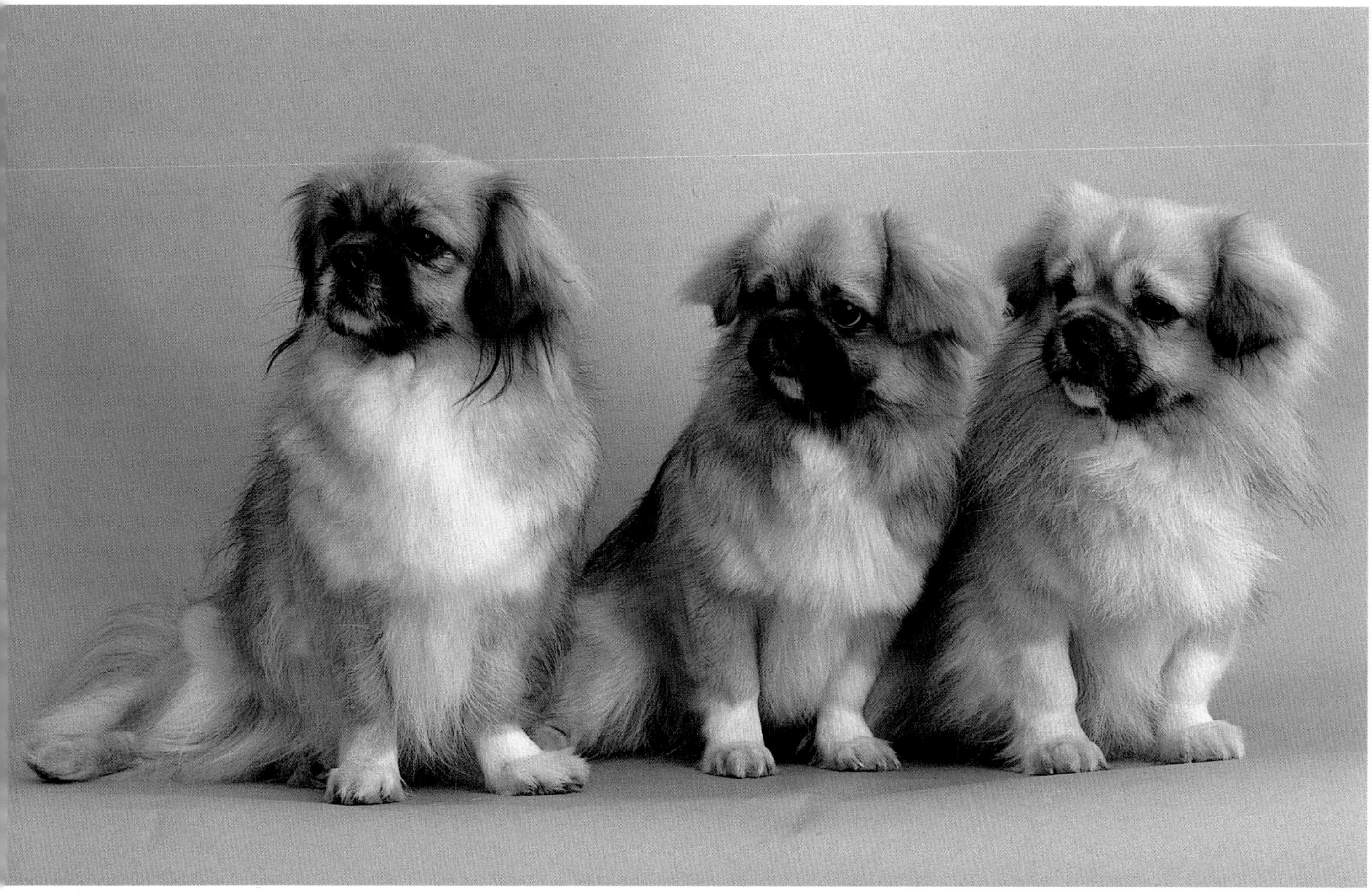

AUTHOR'S ACKNOWLEDGMENTS

Due credit and thanks must go to Paddy Cutts for her patience and hard work in providing a representative selection of photographs in this book.

I would also like to record my grateful thanks to Janet Dodd, Alison Fletcher, Sara-Jane Green and Anne Williams for their help in the production of this book.

Thanks also to the many breeders and exhibitors who gave their time and made their dogs available for studio and location work.

All photographs are by Paddy Cutts/Animals Unlimited.

USEFUL ADDRESSES

American Canine Association
P.O. Box 992
Wilmington, Delaware 19899
(302) 655-3746
1-800-566-6ACA
ACAcanine@aol.com

American Kennel Club
5580 Centerview Drive, Suite 200
Raleigh, North Carolina 27606
(919) 233-9767
www.akc.org.com

ASPCA American Society for Prevention of Cruelty to Animals
424 East 92nd Street
New York, NY 10128-6804
(212) 876-7700

Dog Worldwide-Internet site with veterinarian page, classifieds, chat group, breeds, organizations and clubs, and links to other dog-related sites.
75 South Elliott Road
Chapel Hill, North Carolina 27514
(919) 967-0322
www.dogworldwide.com

Dog Owner's Guide~Comprehensive site with more than 200 articles on dogs, sorted by subject and alphabetically by title.
www.canismajor.com

Good Dog! Magazine~Consumer magazine for dog owners.
P.O. Box 10069
Austin, Texas 78766
www.gooddog@aol.com

Prodogs-Internet site with links to many organizations
www.prodogs.com

Top Dog Endeavors~
The Internet's Most Complete Dog Site
www.tdog.com

U.K.C United Kennel Club, Inc,
100 East Kilgore Road
Kalamzaoo, Michigan 49001-5598
(616) 343-9020

CONTENTS

Introduction 6

Hound Group 8

Sporting Group 48

Terrier Group 88

Nonsporting Group 124

Working & Herding Group 154

Toy Group 212

Index 254

INTRODUCTION

The Canidae—the dog family—includes jackals, wolves, coyotes, dogs, and foxes and is one of eight families in the order Carnivora—the others include bears, raccoons, hyenas and cats. Indeed, until quite recently in evolutionary terms, dogs and cats had not been separated into distinct families. Over the years the felines and the canids became increasingly different, until during the Miocene period they had evolved into quite distinct animals.

The most important step in the evolution of the dog is the appearance of the wolf, descended from animals roaming the Asiatic continent. This was during the last great Ice Age, which ended about 10,000 years ago. Wolves split into various subspecies, and spread throughout Asia and Europe, and into America across the Bering land bridge. The Asiatic and American wolves were not been able to become distinct species because of the link between the two continents; the Bering land bridge ensured a fresh genetic influx, which has had a major influence on how wolves—and dogs—have evolved. Without the link we could have rather different animals in America today.

It is probably from the wolf that man produced the domestic dog, although it is difficult to determine precisely when that happened. However, as a hunting companion, guard, and friend, the working dog quickly became inseparable from man. All over the world man began to breed dogs selectively to perform essential tasks and activities. They became associated with religion: the Pekinese were the temple dogs of China, and the Ancient Egyptians went one step better and venerated Anubis, the jackal god of cemeteries and embalming, and Wapwawet, the jackal-headed god of Upper Egypt.

Selective breeding soon distanced dogs from their wild cousins and today there are more than 400 modern domestic breeds. From early on in the breeding process man identified each breed's essential qualities, and as dogs began to be shown and exhibited—as with so many things, something that was a product of 19th century prosperity—so classification and rules of showing had to be drawn up. It became necessary to organize and codify the optimum features and ways to show them. The organizations that did this tended to be national rather than international—which accounts for the differences encountered around the globe.

There are, unsurprisingly, differences around the world, exemplified by those between the British and American classsification of the groups of dogs: in the UK there are six, in the US seven. Here, because this book originates in Britain, the following group terms are used:

UK term	**US Term**
utility	working
gundog	sporting
hound	hound
terrier	terrier
working	working and herding
toy	toy

Certainly showing today, and the number of breeds that are shown, is growing in popularity. The market for dogs—with a top pedigree or not—has also grown enormously, and dogs are kept as pets all over the world. Prospective owners today, however, need to be able to make a choice from the seemingly myriad breeds: they should be aware of the impact of their purchase—a dog is for life , not just Christmas; small cuddly puppies have a perennial problem—they often turn into 80lb.(30kg) adults, with all the exercising, feeding, grooming, and cleaning that this entails.

The best way to choose the right dog for you is to go to dogshows; talk to breeders and exhibitors; find out the likely size, exercise, and dietary needs; and choose a suitable animal.

This book can help you make your choice: the splendid photographs are divided up by classification, and the development of each group is charted along with a "Points to Remember" section. It is hoped that the book will help the reader make an informed choice and not an impulse purchase.

HOUND GROUP

HOUND GROUP

The Hound group breeds can be broadly divided into sight or scent hounds. The traditional pack breeds, Beagles and Bassets remain popular family pets, as biddable and attractive as they are strong willed on the scent.

Glamorous sight hound of the seventies was the Afghan, a heavily coated breed which requires a great deal of space and exercise.

More suited to the modern pace of life, the Dachshund in all six variations remains popular, particularly the Miniature Smooth and Miniature Longhaired varieties.

Giant of the group is the Irish Wolfhound, almost a metre high (3.03 feet) at the shoulder but a breed with a gentle, kind and friendly nature. Still popular within the group is the Rhodesian Ridgeback, originally bred to assist Rhodesian game hunters in pursuit of their quarry. They remain an excellent, loyal dog and are protective of their family.

A native of Scotland, the Deerhound again has many loyal supporters and remains a great favourite. Elegance, dignity and humour are words which are frequently used to describe this guardian of the baronial fire place.

Regular sight hounds include the Greyhound and Whippet each with its committed devotees. The elegant Saluki has a highly developed hunting instinct and has been acclaimed as the fastest of all dogs.

In recent years the group has been supplemented by the Petit and Grand Basset Griffon Vendéen from France, a rough coated 'basset' type, plus several examples of the Grand variety. Also from France is the similar red wheaten or fawn Basset Fauve de Bretagne.

Sporting breed owners must appreciate the instincts of these majestic dogs.

POINTS TO REMEMBER

All hounds, whether sight or scent, are traditional sporting breeds and so have a strong instinct to pursue. This is sometimes wrongly interpreted as single-mindedness or mischievousness.

Consideration should be given to the size and strength of these dogs. The six varieties of Dachshunds represent the smallest breeds in the group. At the other end of the scale Afghans, Greyhounds, Irish Wolfhounds and Salukis represent the larger varieties which naturally demand more exercise, open spaces and more time.

Hounds are majestic dogs and will repay good care with devotion to the family which is privileged to own them!

The elegant, aloof Afghan Hound. Don't be deceived by that profuse coat, beneath it is a strong and agile sight hound.

Below: Afghan Hound puppies look most appealing in their 'woolly clip' - the makings of the Afghan's fine texture coat.

Right and overleaf: The Basenji (or barkless dog) is renowned for his chortle or yodel and his alert quizzical expression.

The Basenji was also said to have been a palace dog to the Pharaohs of ancient Egypt.

Right: The doleful expression of the long, low Basset Hound breed has great appeal. However, it is a strong, single minded scent hound.

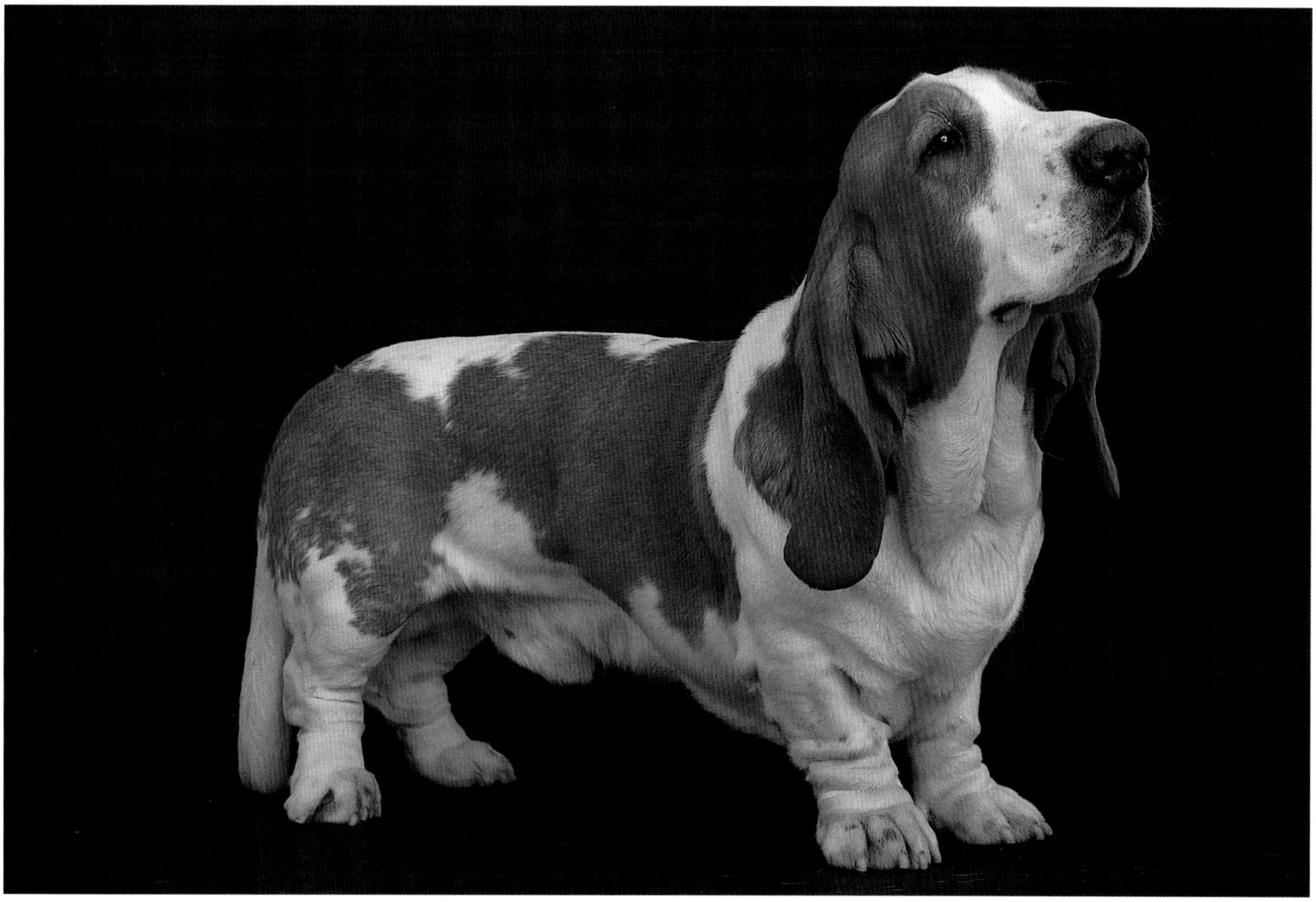

One of the oldest purebred British hounds, the Beagle has become a popular companion in the last 25 years. Its compact appearance and smooth coat make it an attractive hound.

The Borzoi is an old established Russian hunting breed much favoured by the Czars. In 1892 HRH the Grand Duke Nicholas and Prince Oldenbourg entered a team of hounds at Crufts show. On numerous occasions over the course of the next few years the British royal family received these elegant hounds as gifts from their Russian counterparts. A natural sight hound, the Borzoi has a gentle nature, a muscular build and a tremendous turn of speed.

The Miniature Long-haired Dachshunds pictured here show the unusual chocolate dapple (inset) and the attractive pale cream colours of coat. Essentially a hunting dog, they still possess a strong urge to pursue quarry 'to ground'.

This page: The Miniature Wirehaired Dachshunds here show their appealing 'beards' which add character to their expression. The Standard variety of Wirehaired is said to have developed as a result of cross-breeding between the Miniature Schnauzer and the Dandie Dinmont Terrier.

This page: Miniature Smooth-haired Dachshunds showing the popular tan coat (above) and the traditional black and tan variety. Their smooth coats require little grooming.

Overleaf: Eyes left! Typical, quizzical expressions captured by the camera.

Left: The Elkhound is a bold spitz breed, capable of running his quarry for Scandinavian hunters. His dense, soft, woolly undercoat is complemented by a coarse, straight outercoat for warmth and weather resistance in colder climes.

Above: The Finnish Spitz has a distinctive mid length, red-gold or bright reddish brown coat. Its eagerness to hunt is obvious in its alert expression.

In this litter of Finnish Spitz puppies it is easy to see the alert expression and the small, cocked, mobile ears.

Above: The Hamiltonstövare, or Swedish Foxhound, is named after Count Hamilton, the founder of the Swedish Kennel Klub. It is a well proportioned, stylish dog with striking bold tri-colour marking.

Above: The Greyhound is a strong, muscular sight hound, probably the most familiar in this group. A dog of remarkable stamina, it is even-tempered and gentle. The racing 'cousin' to the show dog is out of a slightly smaller mould.

The Irish Wolfhound is the giant of all dogs, with the male standing 81-86 cm (32-34 inches) at the shoulder, and weighing at least 54.5 kgs (109 lbs). Despite their size they have a gentle nature with a soft expression which combines pride with calm.

The Petit Basset Griffon Vendéen is an appealing 'basset type' from Western France. His happy, extrovert character endears him to all.

Above: The Grand variety of the Basset Griffon Vendéen type showing the typical harsh coat and alert expression.

Right: A native of Africa, where it assists big game hunters in running their quarry, the distinctive Rhodesian Ridgeback is a handsome, upstanding dog. The ridge of hair on its back grows in the opposite direction to the body coat.

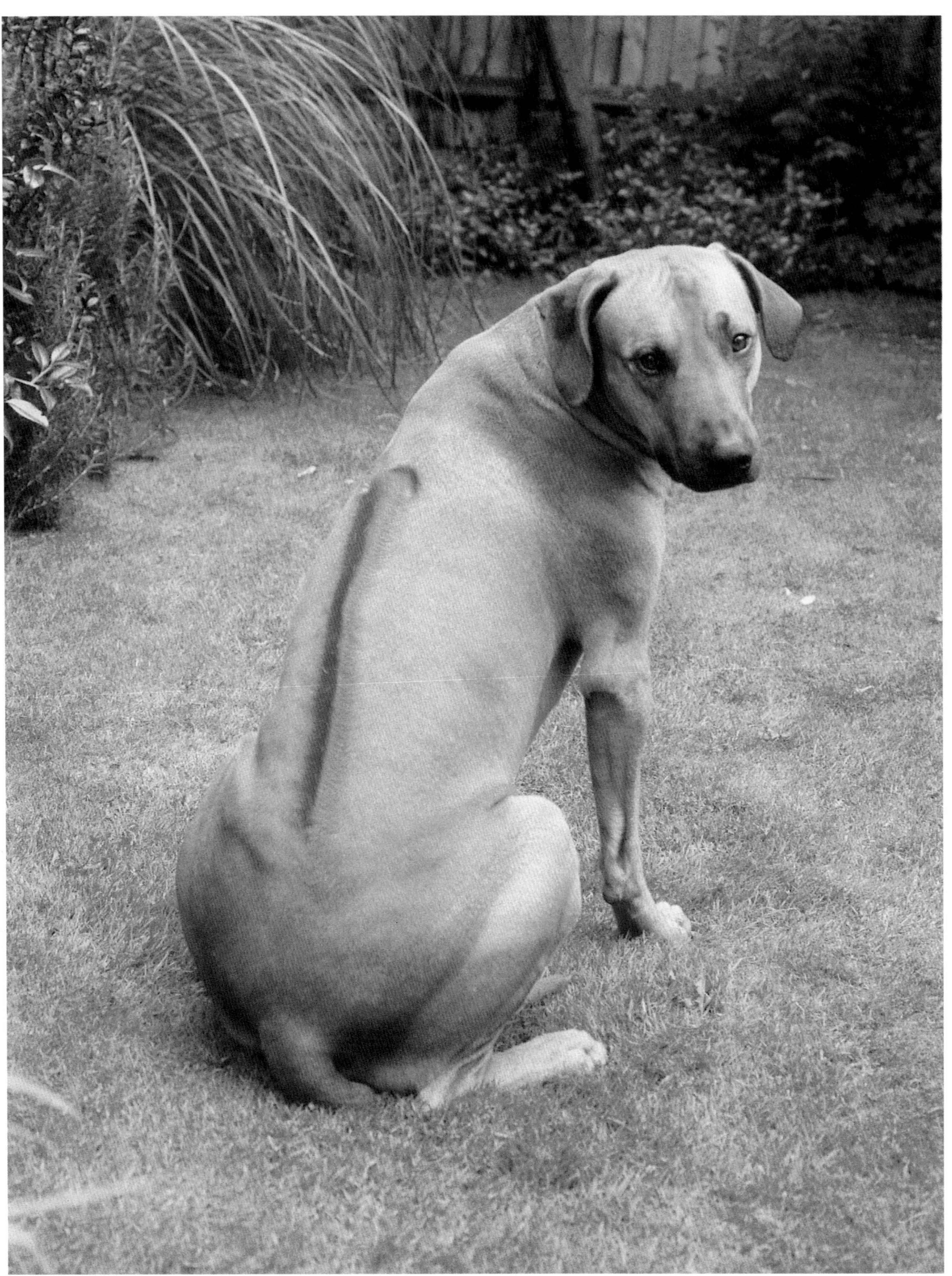

The elegant Saluki can be traced back in time to 329 BC, when it was known to be the domesticated companion to desert tribesmen. Another elegant sight hound, the beautiful ear featherings are displayed to advantage, and note those powerful hindquarters.

Overleaf: This lovely chocolate grizzle colour is sporting a traditional Arabian collar.

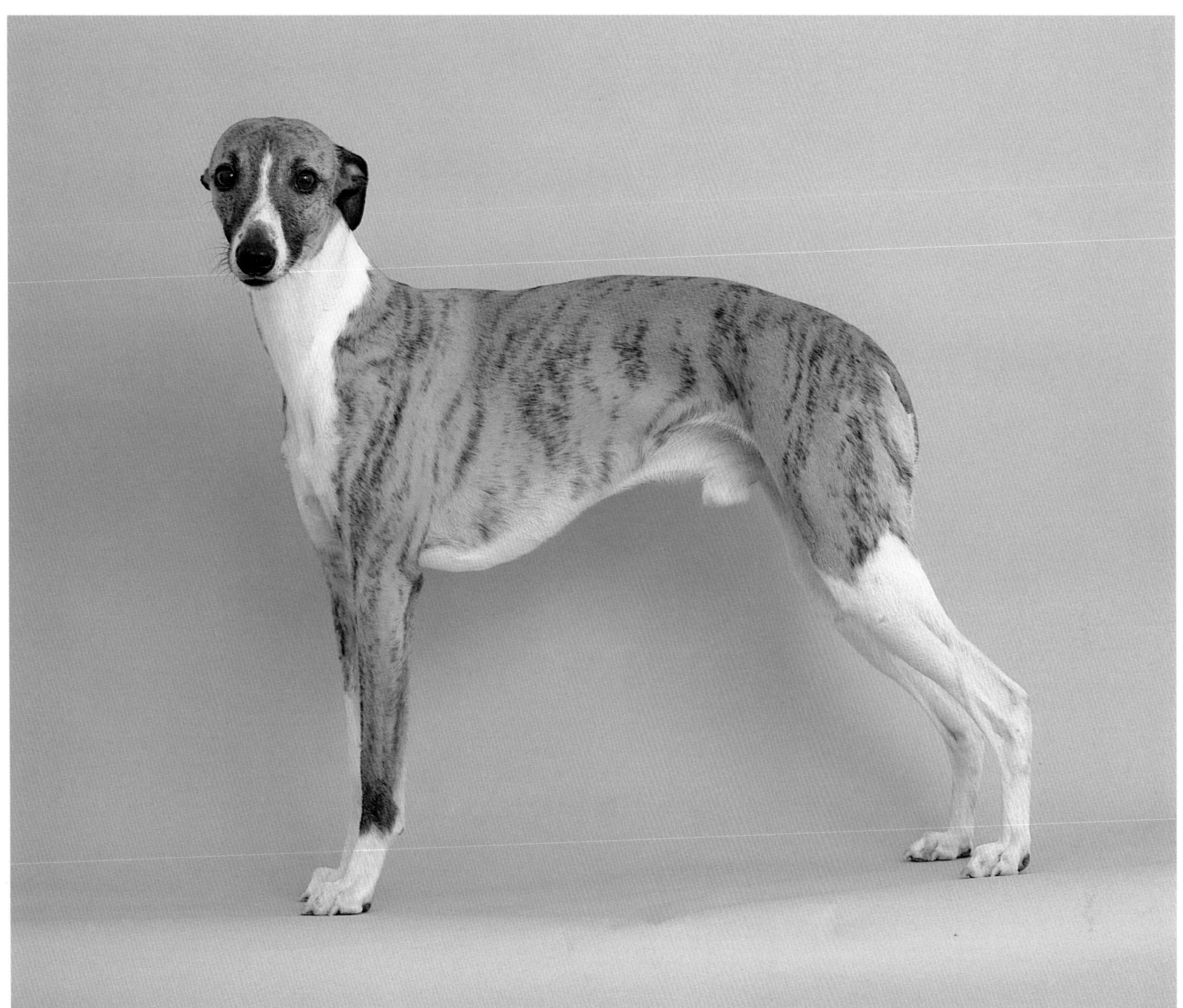

Above and overleaf: The Whippet is a small, muscular hound developed in England and almost certainly evolved from the Greyhound. Whilst Whippet racing was a popular pastime in late Victorian times, the Whippet Club was founded 100 years ago to promote the exhibition of the breed. Many colours and colour combinations are acceptable including this smart tan/brindle and white.

SPORTING GROUP

SPORTING GROUP

The Gundog group includes the firm favourite and currently the most popular of all breeds, the Labrador Retriever.

This all round 'country gentleman' of gundogs has maintained its place in the top ten for many years. Its retrieving ability and intelligence make it a favourite with the shooting fraternity, as a family pet or guide dog for the blind.

The Golden Retriever remains a firm favourite along with the Cocker Spaniel and the English Springer Spaniel.

These two Spaniels are also popular working dogs, although the divide between show and working strains is demonstrated by the smaller, lighter boned 'working cousins'. Nevertheless, their capability should not be underestimated.

'Minor' Spaniel breeds, the Sussex, Field, Clumber, Irish Water and Welsh Springer continue to attract interest, as do the emergent Hunt, Point and Retrieve (HPR) breeds from the continent.

The traditional Pointer, Gordon, English and Irish Setters have been joined by the German Shorthaired and Wirehaired Pointers, Hungarian Vizslas, Italian Spinoni and Weimaraners, which are sometimes described as the 'grey ghost' because of their striking colouration and piercing, light eyes.

The Setters have been re-joined in recent years by the Irish Red and White, a traditional breed out of the same stock as the Irish Setter.

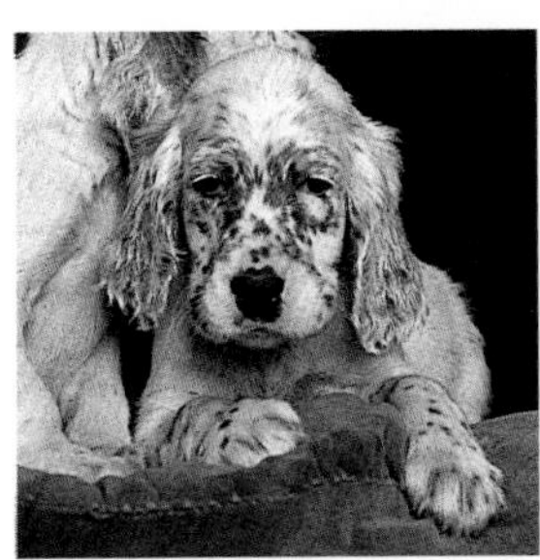

Gundogs need regular exercise and space to run. Their intelligence and willingness to please have to be acknowledged. These sporting dogs usually attract active owners who become committed enthusiasts for life.

POINTS TO REMEMBER

All gundogs are highly intelligent and eager to please.

Their basic instincts to retrieve or 'flush' game are evident in early play and continue to develop. To harness this natural ability demands time and training in their formative months. Consider this when you fall for that adorable bundle of fun.

Properly channelled, this intelligence will produce a sociable, well adjusted dog. Ignore it, as people tend to do with so many breeds, and it will turn to boredom and destructive tendencies.

Consider the size of the adult dogs. For example, the popular Labrador weighs in at 21-31 kilos (60-70 lbs) and can attain half of its adult weight at four months!

Described as the aristocrats of dogs, gundogs deserve space, time and training to realise their full potential. Never underestimate their intelligence.

Right: The English Setter is one of the most glamorous of the Gundogs. His clean outline befits a stylish worker, cheerful companion and elegant mover. The stylish, tireless gait of all the Setters is one of their most attractive features.

Overleaf: An attractive tricolour (blue belton and tan) shown to advantage in a natural situation.

Right and overleaf: The intelligence of the German Shorthaired Pointer is captured in those attractive eyes.

One of the emergent HPR breeds from the Continent, the German Shorthaired Pointer was developed to satisfy the exacting needs of the sportsman and rough-shooter. The popular liver and white ticked colour is shown here.

Above: The German Wirehaired Pointer is making its mark as a medium-sized, all-purpose HPR gundog. The breed is particularly popular with rough shooters for its performance in water and in the field.

Above: The Gordon Setter has distinctive black and tan markings. The breed was developed on the estates of the Dukes of Gordon in Scotland.

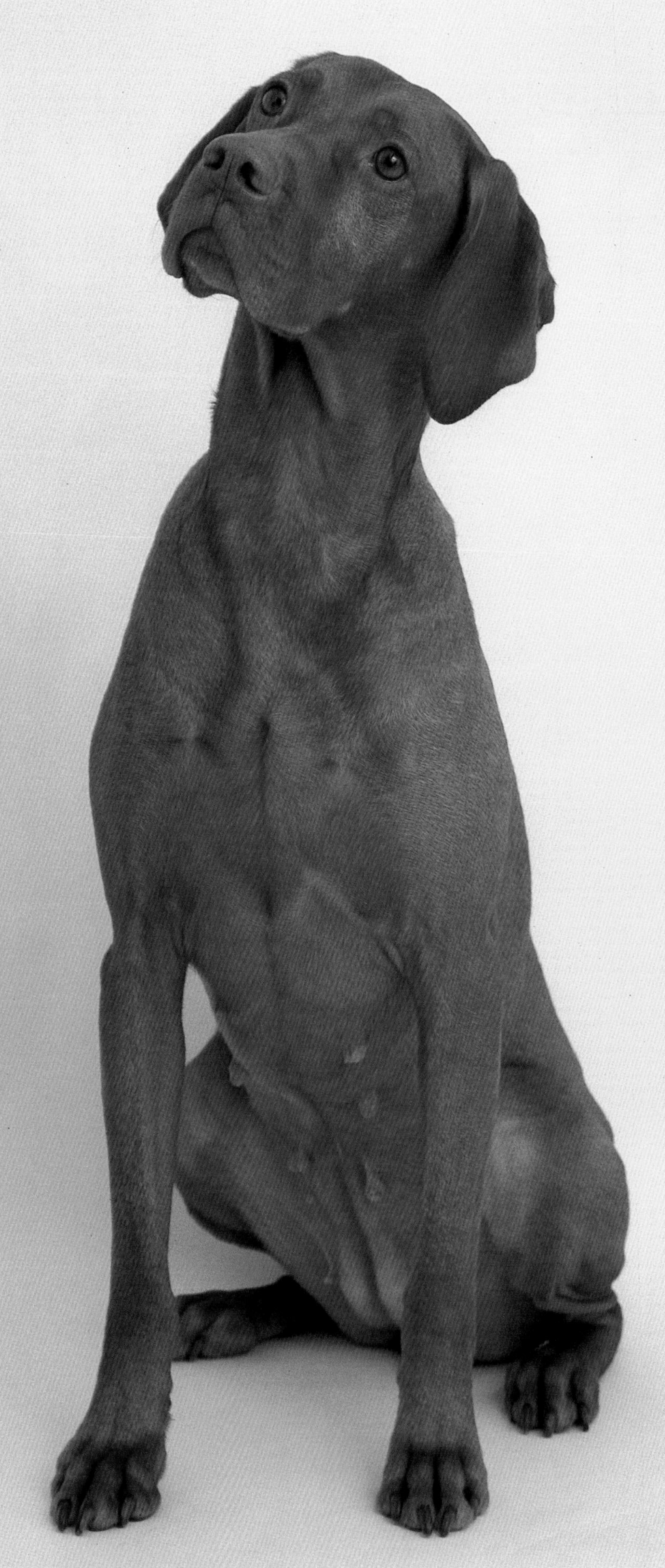

Left: Another continental HPR breed is the Hungarian Vizsla, said to be a close cousin of the Weimaraner and German Shorthaired Pointer. The russet gold coat colour is unique to the breed.

Below and right: The Irish Setter has a magnificent rich chestnut coat and an attractive, elegant outline, making it the most popular of all the Setters. Its handsome, refined good looks belie a devilish sense of humour. Note the slightly greying muzzle of the older dog **(below)**.

The Italian Spinone is thought to have originated in France, but gained popularity in northern Italy's Piedmont region as a sportsman's working companion. It is a big, squarely built dog with well muscled quarters. Here we see the attractive brown roan colouring and **overleaf** the striking orange.

Left: The Large Munsterlander is a medium-sized, multi-purpose continental Gundog, which has enjoyed rising popularity since it was first imported to the UK in the 1970s. Note the eager, alert expression.

Below: The Nova Scotia Duck Tolling Retriever originated from that Canadian province and is one of the smallest retriever breeds. Its thick coat insulates it well from the hostile conditions in which it is expected to work.

A Pointer quartering the ground on moorland eventually coming 'on point' to game is a magnificent sight. They instinctively track and indicate to air scent. The most popular colouring is liver and white, while black and white, orange and white or lemon and white is also acceptable.

Above: The Flatcoated Retriever, or Wavy-coated Retriever as it was known, is an intelligent, medium-sized breed with a distinctive outline. The black **(left)** and liver **(right)** coats shown here are standard coat colours.

Right, opposite and overleaf: The Golden Retriever is another popular breed, whose happy disposition and melting smile have made it a favourite family pet. The 'bundle of fun' puppies become intelligent, confident dogs with natural working ability.

Above: The chocolate coloured Labrador Retriever is much sought after, being a rare coat colour compared to the popular black and yellow shown **overleaf**.

The loyal, biddable and intelligent Labrador Retriever is the most popular of all Gundogs. Beneath its dense outercoat lies a softer, weather resistant undercoat which protects it from extreme cold whilst swimming. The black is favoured by country sportsmen to the equally popular yellow seen in the show ring.

Above and left: The Clumber Spaniel was said to have been bred and developed by the Duke of Newcastle on the Clumber Park estate in Nottinghamshire out of stock imported from France over 200 years ago. This heavy boned Spaniel has its own Working Society dedicated to maintaining high standards in the field.

Right: The 'merry' Cocker is the most popular of all the Spaniel breeds. Always eager to please, its natural retrieving instincts are well known, as is the breed's 'flushing' ability. The breed boasts a range of coat colours, including solid (or self) colours. They enjoy plenty of exercise.

Opposite and left: The English Springer Spaniel is another cheerful extrovert. The oldest of sporting Gundogs, it was used to 'spring' game - hence the name. The breed is a popular family companion and the working strains produce many excellent dogs for the field.

Below and overleaf: Whilst the liver and white is more popular, the black and white is attractive and this one is complete with an undocked tail since the practice of tail docking for cosmetic reasons by persons other than vets was banned in the UK in 1993.

Above: A coat of tight ringlets makes the Irish Water Spaniel distinctive amongst the Spaniels. Dark liver in colour, the coat protects the tallest of the Spaniel family in the water. A versatile gundog, it is an excellent retriever and much favoured by wildfowlers.

The Sussex Spaniel is one of Britain's traditional minor spaniel breeds originating from the county on the south coast which boasted huge sporting estates in the 18th century. The correct coat colour is described as 'rich golden liver'. Although not a speedy spaniel, its typical movement has a distinctive roll and its scenting ability equals that of other sporting spaniels.

The Weimaraner, or 'grey ghost', is another continental multi-purpose HPR breed specifically developed by the Dukes of the Weimar Republic to meet their exacting standards. Its striking colouration, light eyes and fearless but friendly temperament have endeared it to enthusiasts over the last 25 years.

TERRIER GROUP

TERRIER GROUP

The Terrier group's most popular breed is the West Highland White Terrier, a 'game' little dog with personality plus.

Like most of the terriers, his harsh coat requires regular care and attention. His close Highland associates, the Cairn, Scottish and Skye Terriers also remain firm favourites.

Completing the quintet from Scotland is the Dandie Dinmont, named after the much vaunted character in Sir Walter Scott's *Guy Mannering*. His soulful expression belies a workmanlike Terrier.

The Staffordshire Bull Terrier remains a firm favourite - witness the crowd several deep around the ringside at any Crufts show! Despite his historical link with fighting, his affectionate nature and love of family life and children are widely acknowledged.

The list of 26 breeds in this group reads like a regional map of Britain with the popular Border Terrier a recent addition to the top 10 all breeds list.

Originating from the border region between England and Scotland, it is described as essentially a working terrier capable of going to ground after foxes.

The Bedlington, which bears a strong resemblance to a lamb, is another sporting north country dog.

From Ireland we have the Kerry Blue, the Irish, the Glen of Imaal and the

Soft-coated Wheaten Terrier, a medium-sized dog with an unusually soft and silky coat.

Traditional 'English' and popular breeds must include the Bull Terrier, its miniature cousin and the Wire and Smooth Fox Terrier. 'King' of the Terriers is the majestic Airedale, standing up to 61cm (25 in) at the shoulder.

A later addition to the group in 1990 was the Parson Jack Russell, a breed based on the type favoured by the hunting Devon parson, the Reverend John Russell.

British-bred terriers are in great demand the world over, and recent years have seen a healthy growth in the import and export of stock to the advantage of many breeds.

POINTS TO REMEMBER

A well-known judge once told me to remember that all terriers believe they are twice their actual size.

Their popularity in the top 20 breeds cannot be denied, with West Highland Whites, Cairns and Staffords as popular as ever.

The indomitable terrier spirit endears them to family life as does their size, the majority of the 26 breeds in the group being short-legged. Regular brushing of any dog is essential and in terriers coat care must go one step further with 'stripping' (removal of surplus coat hair, fringes and feathering) if the correct texture and colour is to be maintained.

Terriers are sporting dogs with a tendency to chase and 'go to ground' if allowed. However, their larger than life personality and size make them a popular choice as a family pet.

Affectionately known as the 'King of Terriers' the Airedale was recognised as a pedigree breed in 1879. It was thought to be an amalgam of Harrier, Otterhound and Old English Terrier in its native Yorkshire. As with many terrier breeds, its coat requires careful attention.

Careful coat trimming has maintained the correct outline of this Airedale dog.

The Australian Terrier is a strong, rugged character and is essentially a working dog. He is a friendly extrovert with a harsh coat and alert expression. Note the harsh, dense, straight topcoat giving way to the underbody coat.

The Bedlington's lamb-like appearance belies a tough, graceful and muscular dog. He has a distinctive blue liver or sandy coloured coat and a light springy gait when walking.

Right: One of the most popular of Terriers, the Border is a natural looking worker, capable of doing a day's work in the field. It has a harsh, dense coat and close undercoat.

Below: The Bull Terrier is a strongly built, four square Terrier. Traditionally all white in colour, they are also common in brindle, red, fawn and tri-colour.

The Cairn is one of the most popular of the terrier breeds with its mischievous expression and harsh texture coat. A native of Scotland, it is described as strong, compact and workmanlike. Above is a grey brindle and, right and left, an attractive head study of a cream.

Above and right: The Smooth Fox Terrier is another of Britain's traditional breeds, which, along with the Wire Fox, was the most popular of terrier breeds over 100 years ago. As a hunting breed this breed has a lively, gay disposition.

Left: The Dandie Dinmont is one of Scotland's traditional breeds. Note the distinctive head, silky hair on the domed skull and those wise, intelligent eyes.

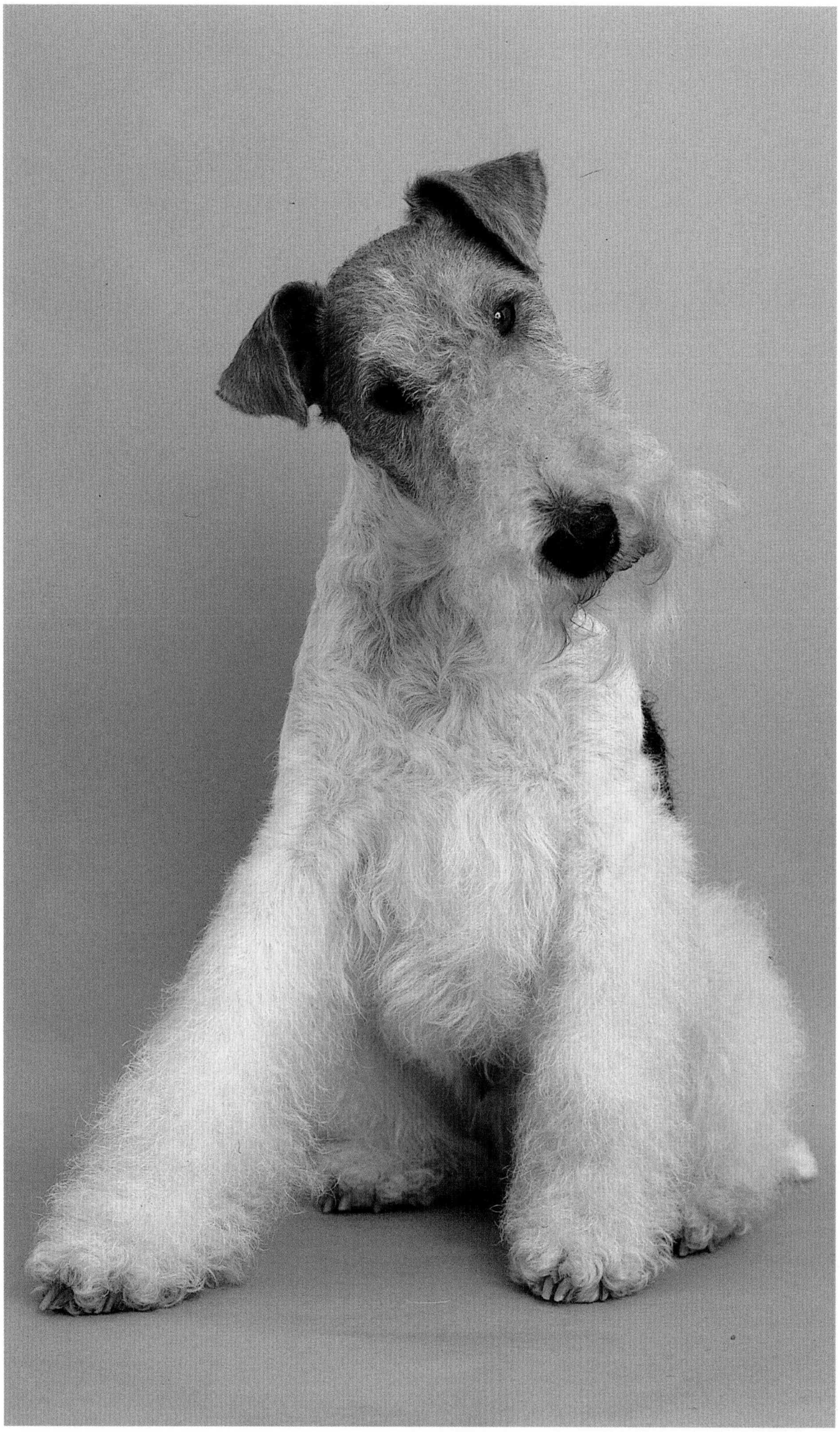

The Wire Fox Terrier overtook its Smooth cousin in popularity until in Britain, in 1913, its own 'Wire' association catered for enthusiasts. As it is a 'coated' breed, due care and attention should be given to those furnishings so well illustrated here.

The Kerry Blue is noted for its steel blue coat and dark points. A compact, medium-sized terrier, it continues to attract good entries at principal shows.

Above: Derived from the Black and Tan Terrier of the 19th century, the Manchester is a keen, alert sporting companion. Its jet black coat is tipped with rich mahogany, noticable in this photograph on the muzzle and forelegs.

Right and opposite: The Norfolk and its close cousin, the Norwich, are typical short-legged Terriers. When trying to distinguish between the two breeds, the ears are the key - Norfolks **(illustrated here)** have ears which drop forward, whilst the Norwich sports alert-looking, erect ears.

The traditional Parson Jack Russell Terrier gained Kennel Club recognition in 1990. Developed by the Reverend John Russell, the breed type now closely resembles the type much favoured by the famous hunting West Country parson.

The Scottish Terrier is a firm favourite amongst the traditional Scottish breeds. Bold but not aggressive, it is a loyal and faithful friend. Don't be deceived by those chocolate-box looks.

Left: The Staffordshire Bull Terrier is a smooth coated, agile dog for its medium to small size. It is noted for its intelligence and affectionate nature, particularly towards children.

Below and overleaf: The Welsh Terrier is a smart, compact breed, sometimes described as an Airedale in miniature, whereas its nearest cousin is the Lakeland. The breed was in the limelight in 1994 when a top winning specimen was best in show at Crufts.

Right and overleaf: Without doubt the most popular of Terriers, the West Highland White has remained a firm favourite, with two excellent examples of the breed going on to win best in show at Crufts in recent years.

NONSPORTING GROUP

NONSPORTING GROUP

For its size the Utility group has considerable 'Best in show' success at championship level.

It boasts the flamboyant and immaculately presented Poodle in its three varieties; the most popular breeds in the group are the Shih Tzu, an ancient breed of Tibetan origin, its close cousin the Lhasa Apso, a breed greatly improved by imported stock from the USA and the ever popular Dalmatian with its distinctive liver or black spots.

The traditional British breed, the Bulldog, is now overshadowed by the overseas additions to the group.

From the far east the popular Japanese Akita now accounts for a reasonable number of registrations, along with its compatriots the Japanese Shiba Inu and Japanese spitz. The Akita is the powerful, majestic national dog of Japan, the Shiba, another sturdy spitz, is a smaller dog, the popularity of which has escalated in the last 10 years.

Also from the orient is the familiar Chow Chow, a breed which features in Chinese art dating back over 2,000 years. More recently the popular Shar Pei has come to the fore during the last 20 years. Here, once again, both breeds share the same ancestors.

The Utility group also includes additional breeds from the continent in the shape of the German spitz (Klein and Mittel), adding greater weight to the possibility of a separate Spitz group in years to come.

At present the spitz types of breeds are distributed amongst the Toy, Utility, Working and Hound groups and there is a strong case for combining these to form one single group.

Twenty years ago there were only 15 breeds in the Utility group, whereas it now embraces 24 very diverse breeds.

POINTS TO REMEMBER

This group contains a wide variety of different breeds. The largest is the Standard Poodle and amongst the smallest its Toy 'cousin', the German Spitz (Klein) and the popular Shih Tzu.

Many of these are breeds with a profuse coat in the correct show trim, but which demand considerable care and attention if they are to remain attractive. The spitz breeds in particular share a distinctive thick 'stand off' coat which is part of their charm.

The group also includes the Bulldog, a firm favourite, the Dalmatian and French Bulldogs - all smooth coated breeds. Close care and attention must be given to selection when considering ownership of the widely diverse characters in this group.

The Bulldog is descended from the 19th century bull-baiting dogs. Now a thickset, four-square breed its appearance has been carefully maintained. It is single minded to the point of obstinacy, so enthusiasts have to be committed!

Chow Chows originate from the orient, where they were used as a guard dog. They are a broad-chested, muscular dog with an unusual blue tongue. Note the thick coat on this comparatively young dog pictured **below right**.

Left: The Dalmatian, a native of central Europe, was bred and kept as a 'carriage' dog in the 18th century to protect those on long journeys from attack by wolves. Its distinctive spotting in black or liver should be evenly distributed on a white coat.

Below: The Japanese Spitz is a small spitz type which has become popular in recent years. The 'stand-off' pure white coat gives way to a thick undercoat, both of which need care and attention.

The Keeshond is another spitz type with a profuse, harsh coat and dense ruff shown to advantage here. The tail carriage should be close and held over the body **(overleaf)**.

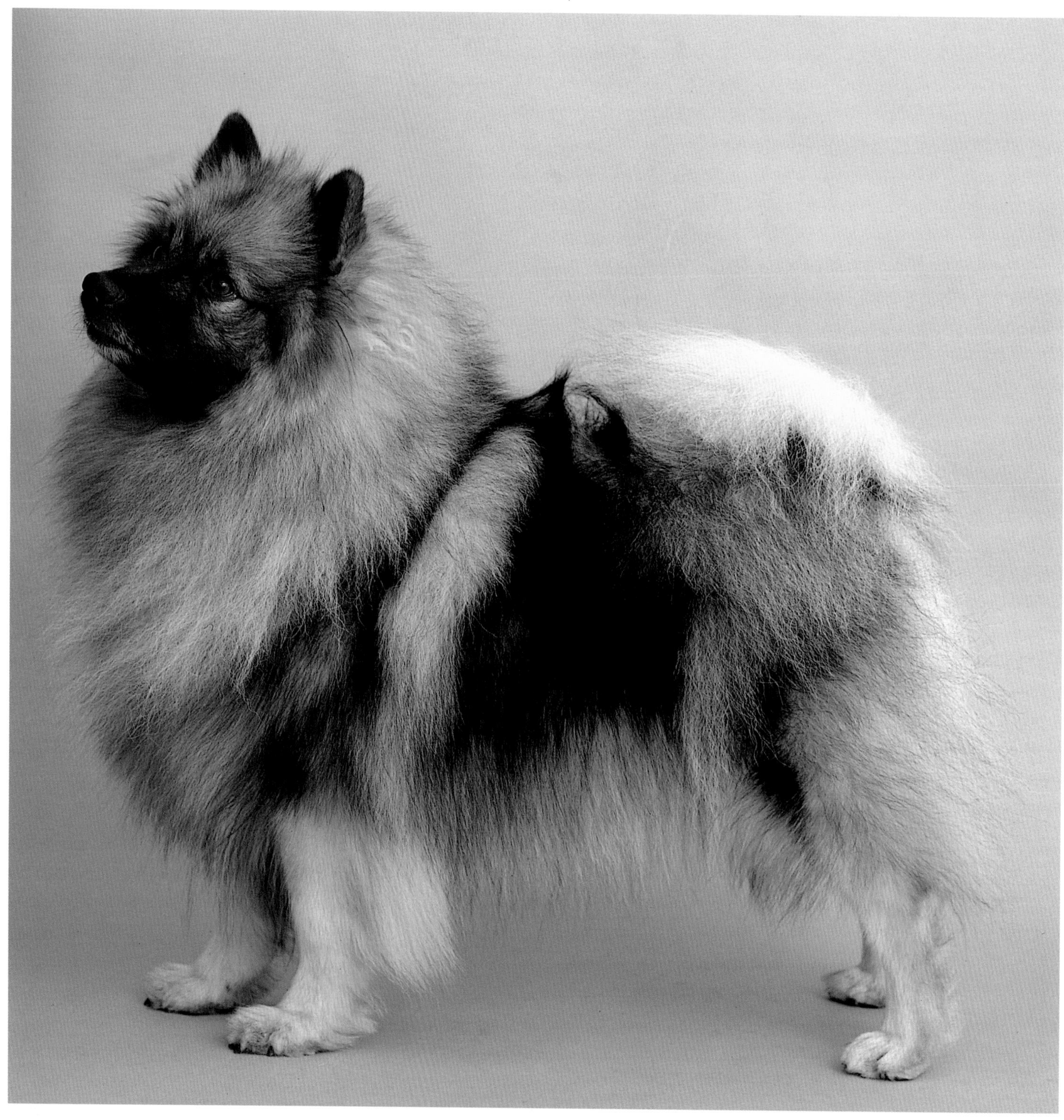

Right: The Lhasa Apso was introduced to Britain in 1928 and it is one of several Tibetan breeds. Popular and successful bloodlines now exist in Britain, America and Scandinavia.

Acceptable Lhasa Apso colouring includes the smoke and white pictured on the preceding page and opposite showing a good outline, and the appealing sandy/gold pictured above.

The Poodle in its Standard form was originally a gundog worked extensively in western Europe but originating from France. Sporting dogs had a full coat but would have their hindquarters clipped to enable them to swim in pursuit of game. Such clipping is thought to have given rise to the fashionable way in which the ladies of the Montmartre presented the Miniature and Toy Poodles which descended from the Standard.

Below: The Schnauzer family originates from Germany. These dogs were bred mainly as 'yard' dogs and to cut down vermin. The Miniature illustrated here shows off the breed's hard textured and wiry coat.

Right: The Schipperke, or Barge Dog, is just that - a small breed developed to act as a guard on the canal boats on Flemish canals. His name in Flemish means "little captain" which refers as much to his self-importance as to his nautical air!

Maintaining the far eastern theme, the Shih Tzu harks from China and is often confused with the Lhasa. The coat is long and dense and on this page we see a gold and white and a black and white, groomed in a more natural style.

Above: This gold and white Shih Tzu shows off the heavily plumed tail correctly carried over the back.

Right and overleaf: The Tibetan Spaniel is a native of the roof of the world, where it is a dog with great status due to its religious significance. Kept in monasteries and temples, it is often the only animal allowed in such holy places. It has enjoyed increased popularity in the UK over the last 50 years.

Right and overleaf: The Tibetan Terrier, which is not classified as a terrier breed, is another product of close breeding in the monasteries of Tibet, to produce a singular type. Sometimes compared to the Old English Sheepdog in miniature, the breed has a profuse, wavy or straight top coat and all colours except chocolate or liver are permissable.

WORKING & HERDING GROUP

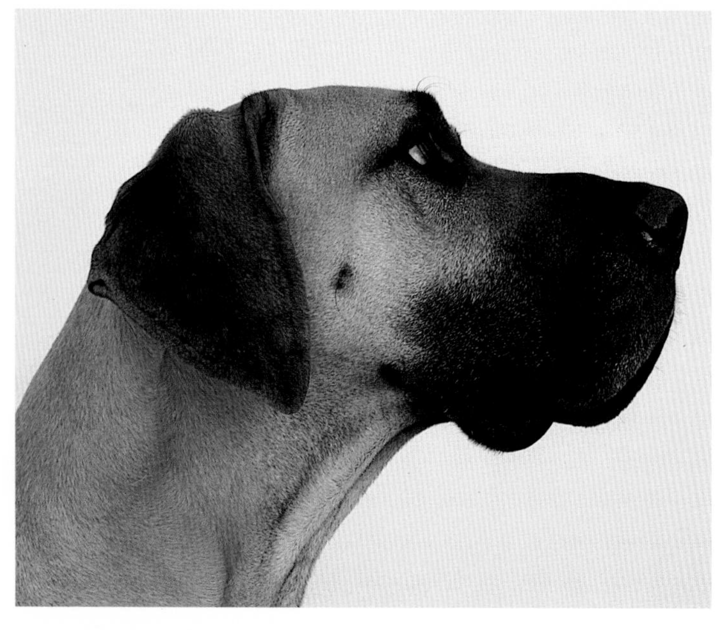

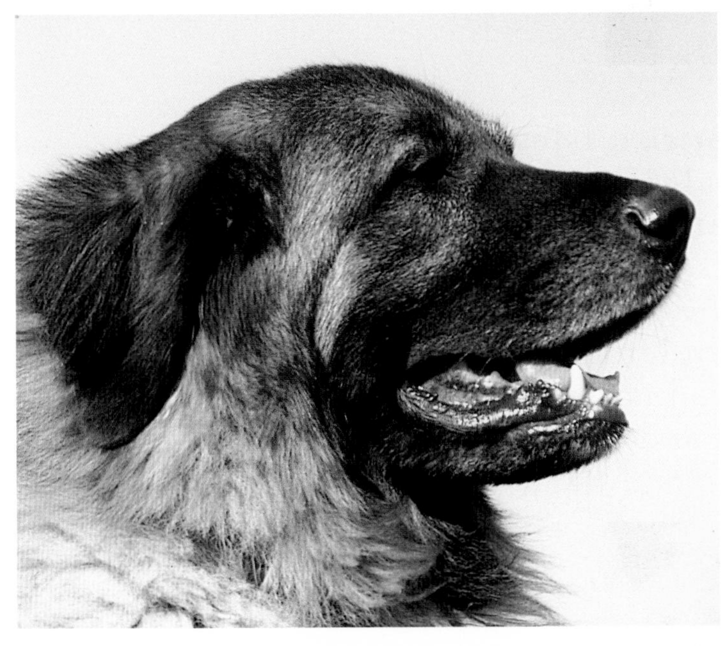

WORKING & HERDING GROUP

The 50 breeds in the Working group include all the pastoral and flock guarding breeds.

Breeds native to the British Isles include the Collie type in all its varieties. Scotland is justified in its claim that it developed these breeds, although a fairly recent addition to the group, and the show ring, was the Border Collie. This highly intelligent breed is still actively worked in obedience and agility alike.

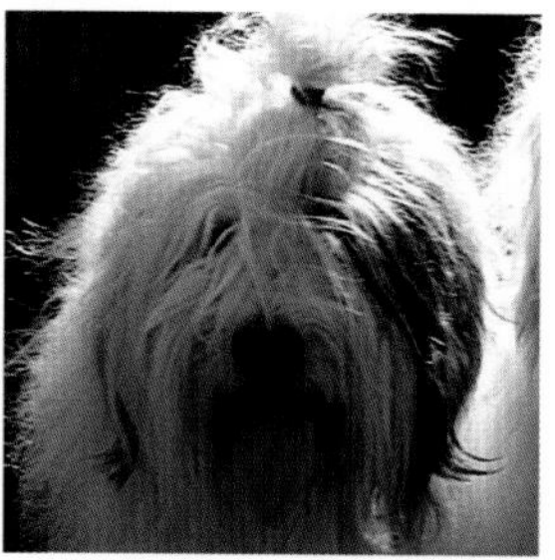

Other native types include the popular Old English Sheepdog, the more obscure but recently revived Lancashire Heeler and the Welsh Corgi in the Pembroke and Cardigan varieties.

This breed was inter-bred until the early 1930s, when separate classification was scheduled at shows.

The German Shepherd continues to attract its enthusiasts and maintains pole position in the popularity stakes.

Second place goes to the Boxer, with an almost equal third slot going to the Rough Collie and the Shetland Sheepdog.

A whole range of draught dogs from the lowlands and central Europe now dominates a group which was created in 1963 when the non-sporting breeds were split to form the Utility and Working groups.

Add to these the striking Australian Cattle Dog from down under, the Swedish Lapphund and Vallhund, the almost Poodle-like Portuguese Water Dog, the famous and much loved St. Bernard and the Mastiff and mollosoid types from Italy and Tibet, and it is easy to see what a cosmopolitan group this is!

Once again here is a group under close scrutiny and ripe for partition into pastoral or shepherding breeds sections.

POINTS TO REMEMBER

Over 50 breeds make up the 'Working' element and here we have the largest group with the largest dogs.

Space, time and exercise are essentials when considering ownership of any breed in this group. There are few short-legged examples and most have the profuse coat typical of pastoral and flock guarding breeds from hostile climates.

Some of the shepherding breeds have a thick double coat which requires special care and attention, particularly after exercising in wet weather.

Along with size this group can lay claim to brains as well, for many of its breeds also acquit themselves well in obedience, working trials and agility.

The Alaskan Malamute is regarded as the national breed of Alaska. Immensely powerful, it is a natural sled dog and faithful companion.

The Australian Cattle Dog is the product of imported stock and carries the bloodlines of several working breeds. Note the inquisitive, intelligent expression, large fox-like ears, and 'brush' of a tail.

The Bearded Collie was only recognised as an individual breed 50 years ago but its roots go back over a century to Scotland and the collie-types bred for their intelligence and herding abilities. Alert, lively and self-confident, its slate grey, reddish fawn or brown coat demands close attention.

The Belgian Shepherd Dog in all its four varieties is a herding dog of lowland Europe. The three main varieties vary in coat colour with the Laekenois **(right)** having a distinctive harsh, wiry, reddish fawn coat. The Kennel Club has now decided to recognise all four varieties as one breed.

Within the Belgian Shepherd fraternity enthusiasts still advocate the individual varieties such as the all black Groenendael **(page 166)**, the Tervueren **(left)** and the black masked Malinois **(right)**.

Left: Described as every child's idea of what a dog should look like, the Bernese Mountain Dog hails from the Bernese Oberland region of Switzerland. Used as a draught dog on hill farms, it has an impeccably good nature and friendly character.

Right and below: Recognised as the world's finest sheepdog, the Border Collie has its origins in the hills of Scotland. The considerable success achieved by the breed at Obedience and Working Trial level resulted in growing interest in the breed as a show dog, and in Kennel Club registration in the 1980s.

Above: The Bouvier des Flandres is a powerfully built drover's dog from the low countries which was used extensively as a messenger or ambulance dog in the First World War. His tough, wiry outcoat has a fine, soft undercoat.

Below and overleaf: The popular Boxer is another Germanic breed, the name of which is derived from the way it punches the air in play. Devotees appreciate its biddable, fearless temperament and here we see good examples of the brindle/white and red/white colouring.
In the USA, the American Kennel Club requires Boxers being shown to have their ears docked.

Right and overleaf: The Briard is an ancient 'Berger' sheepdog from the continent which, despite achieving some popularity in the UK 100 years ago, has only increased in numbers in the last 15 years. Here we see some fine examples of the black and fawn shading in its profuse coat.

Below and overleaf: The Bullmastiff is a popular and slightly smaller version of the traditional Mastiff from which it was derived. It was used as a guard by gamekeepers to protect their masters' estates from poachers.

Above: As one of Scotland's traditional herding breeds the Rough Collie was admired by Queen Victoria in the 1860s on one of her first visits to the Balmoral estates. Her love of the breed assured its future popularity. This blue merle has the permitted blue or blue flecked eyes.

The origins of the Dobermann Pinscher can be traced back to the 1860s and a German tax collector, Herr Louis Dobermann, who wanted a dog for protection on his rounds. Thought to have been crossed with a pinscher or terrier type, the Dobermann is a stylish, loyal companion which needs firm handling.

Above: The Eskimo Dog is a powerfully built, heavy coated breed and, as the name implies, the haulage dog of the Eskimo tribe. It has terrific stamina and a thick double coat to enable it to survive the worst Arctic conditions.

Right: The Estrela Mountain Dog from Portugal is typical of many European herding and guarding breeds. Note the deep chest and broad, massive head of this powerful breed.

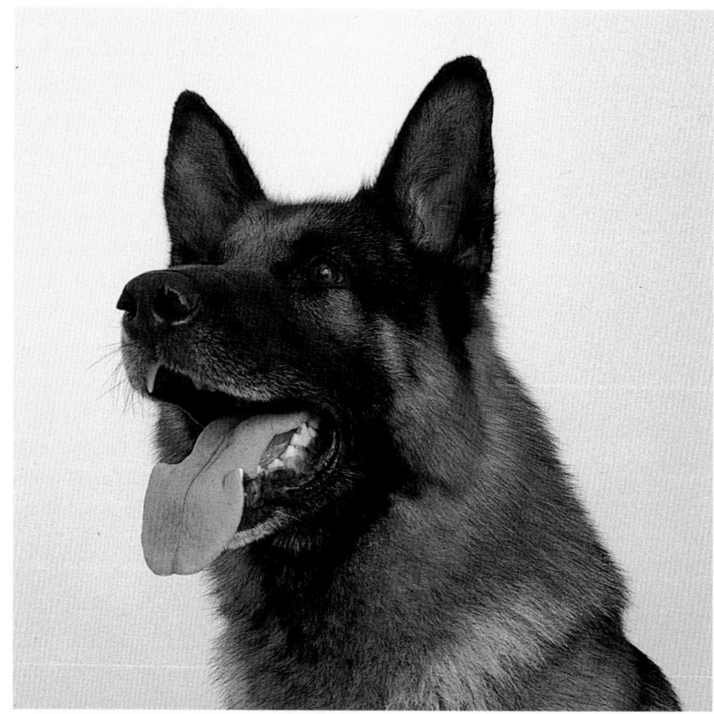

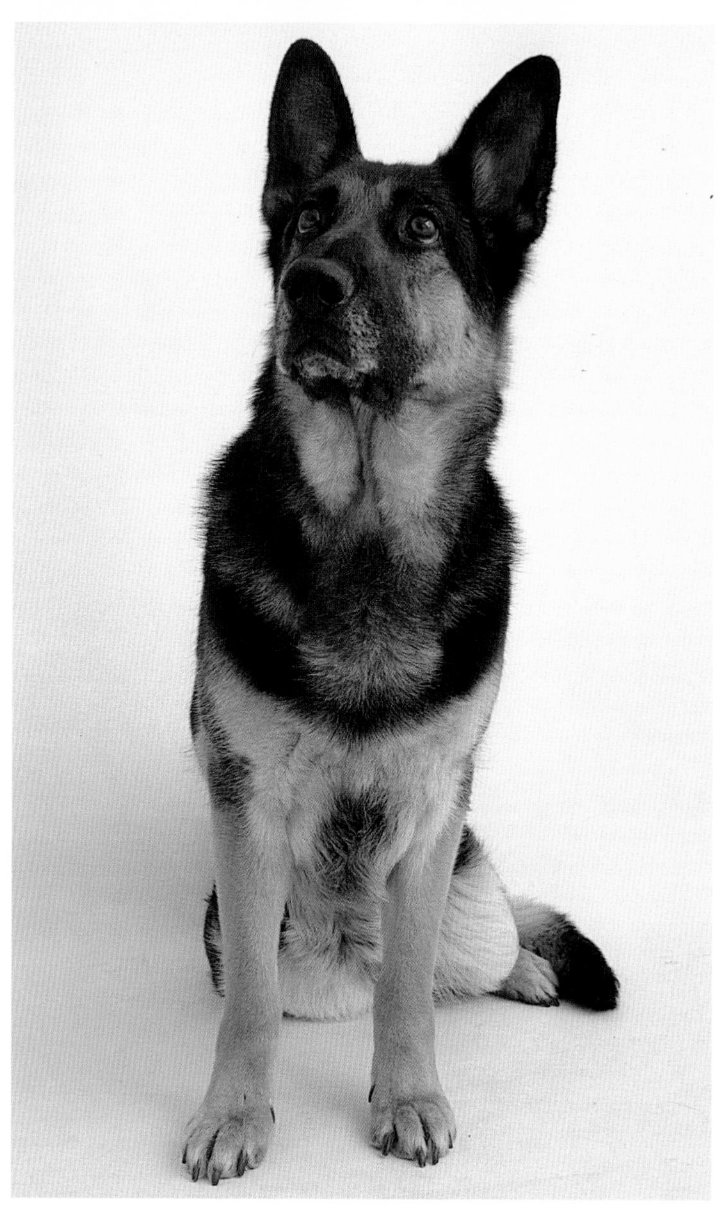

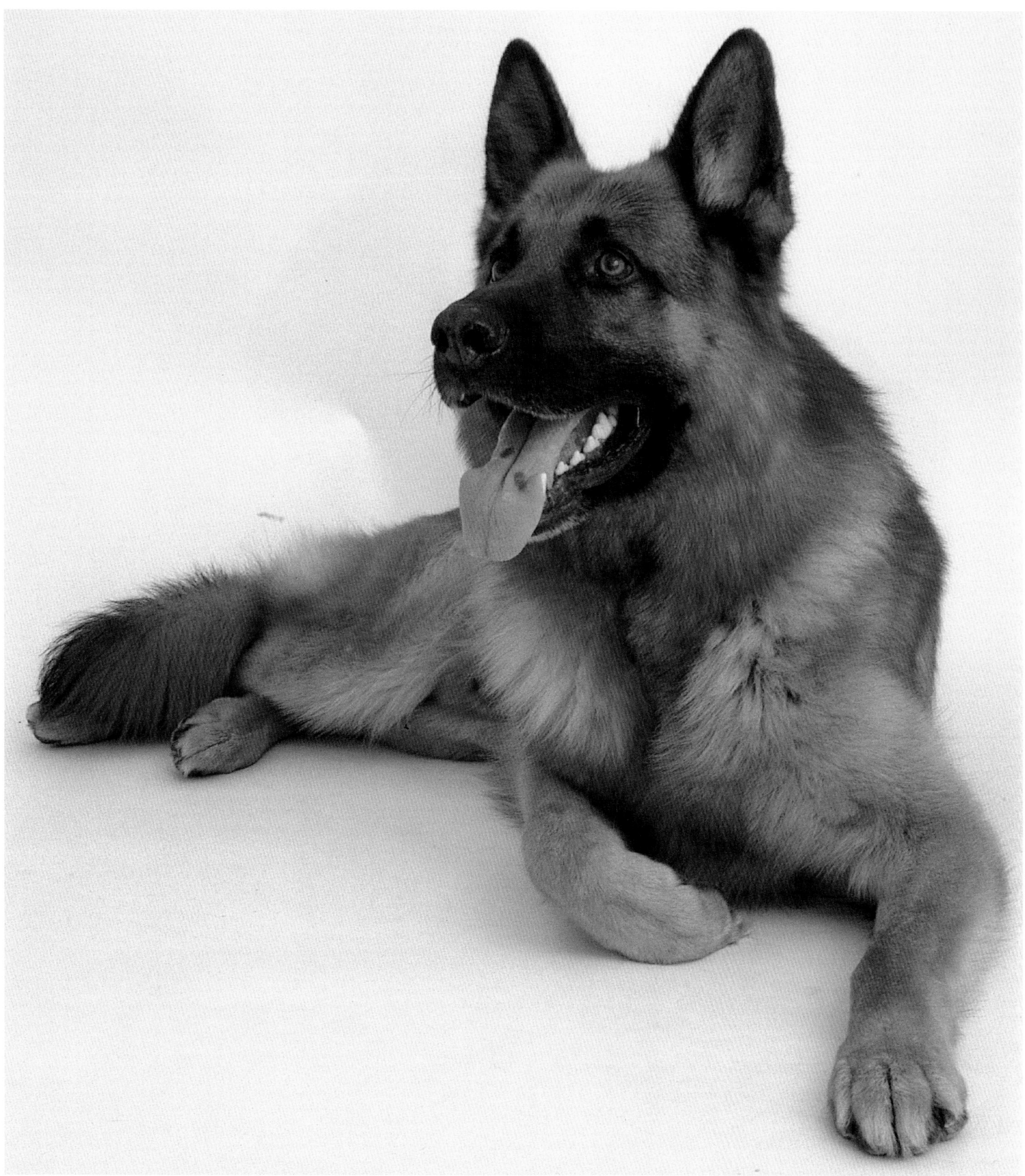

The German Shepherd Dog was the most popular dog in Britain in 1926 when it was known as the Alsatian Wolf Dog. Its qualities were appreciated by soldiers in the First World War in which it was used as an ambulance and messenger dog in front lines. Undoubtedly the most popular breed worldwide, with distinguished service in the police and the armed services, it has a loyal following of enthusiasts. Known as the Alsatian until the early 1970s, German Shepherd bloodlines have definite English and German types. Recent years have seen increased interest in the importation of continental stock which has made its mark in the showring today. Note the alert expression of this versatile working dog.

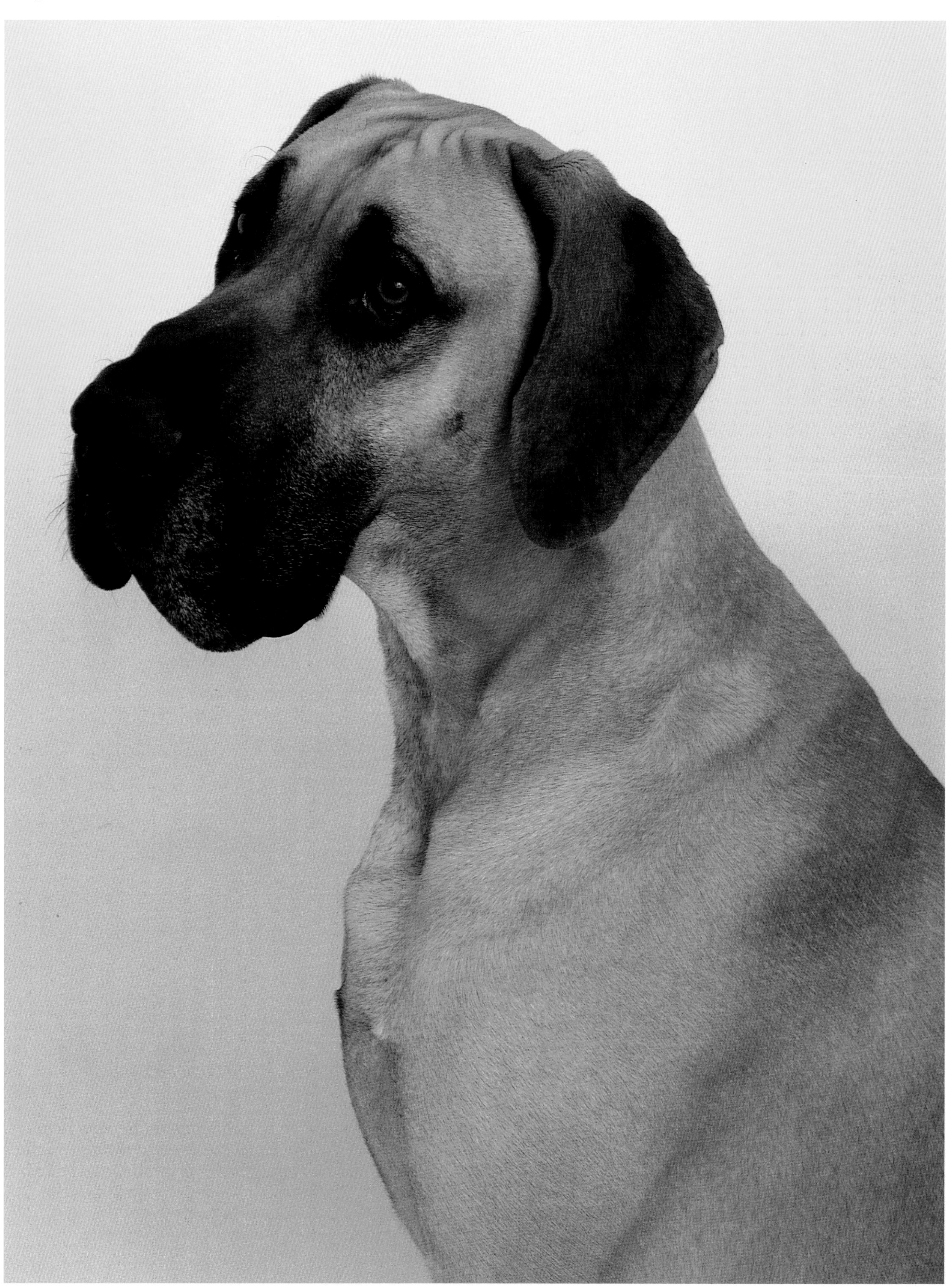

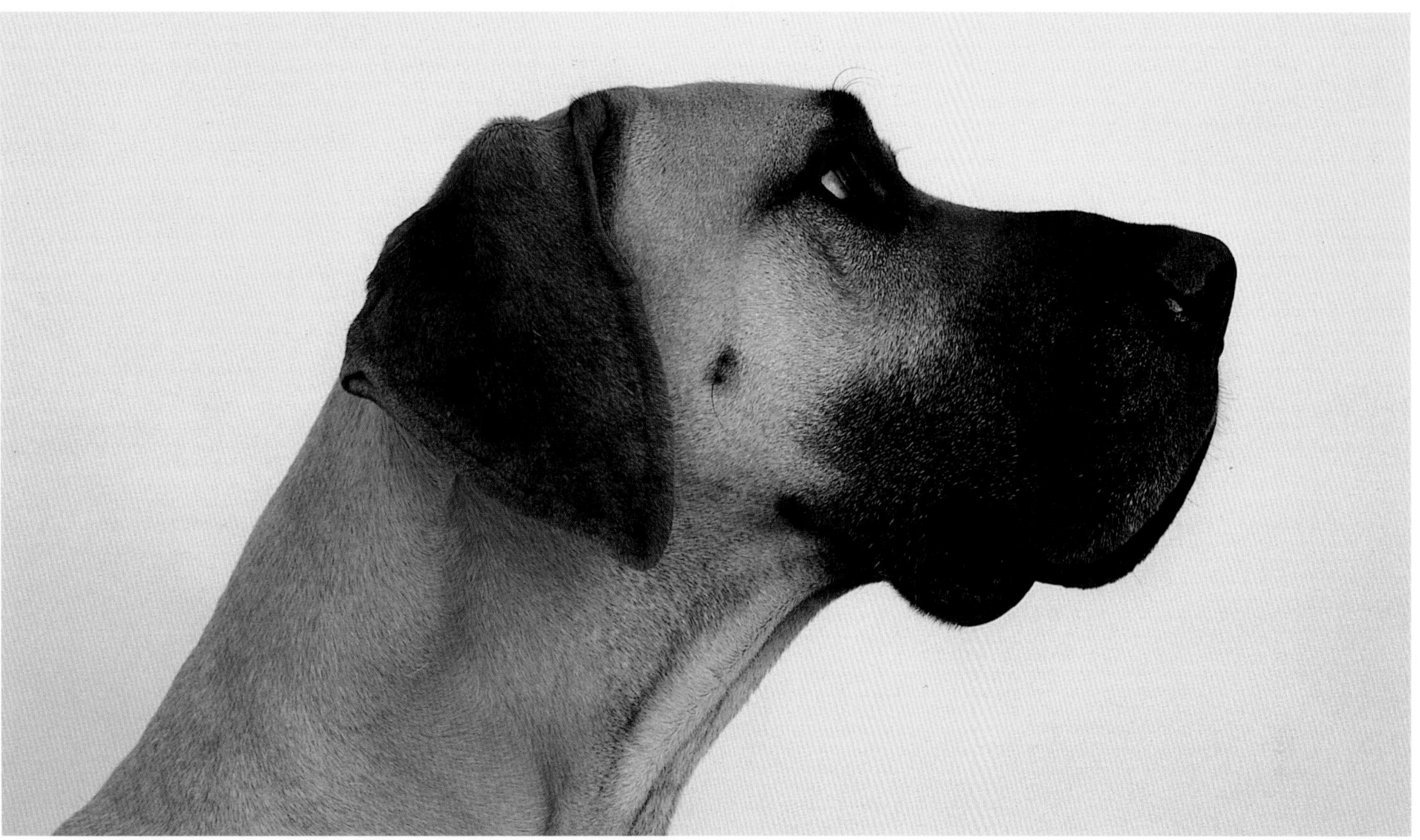

The popular Great Dane is of German origin and was used in the 17th century as a coursing and hunting dog. The breed today is much finer in bone and body but an adult male can weigh in at 54 kg (120 lbs). The popular fawn with black mask is shown here with the striking harlequin **(below and overleaf)**.

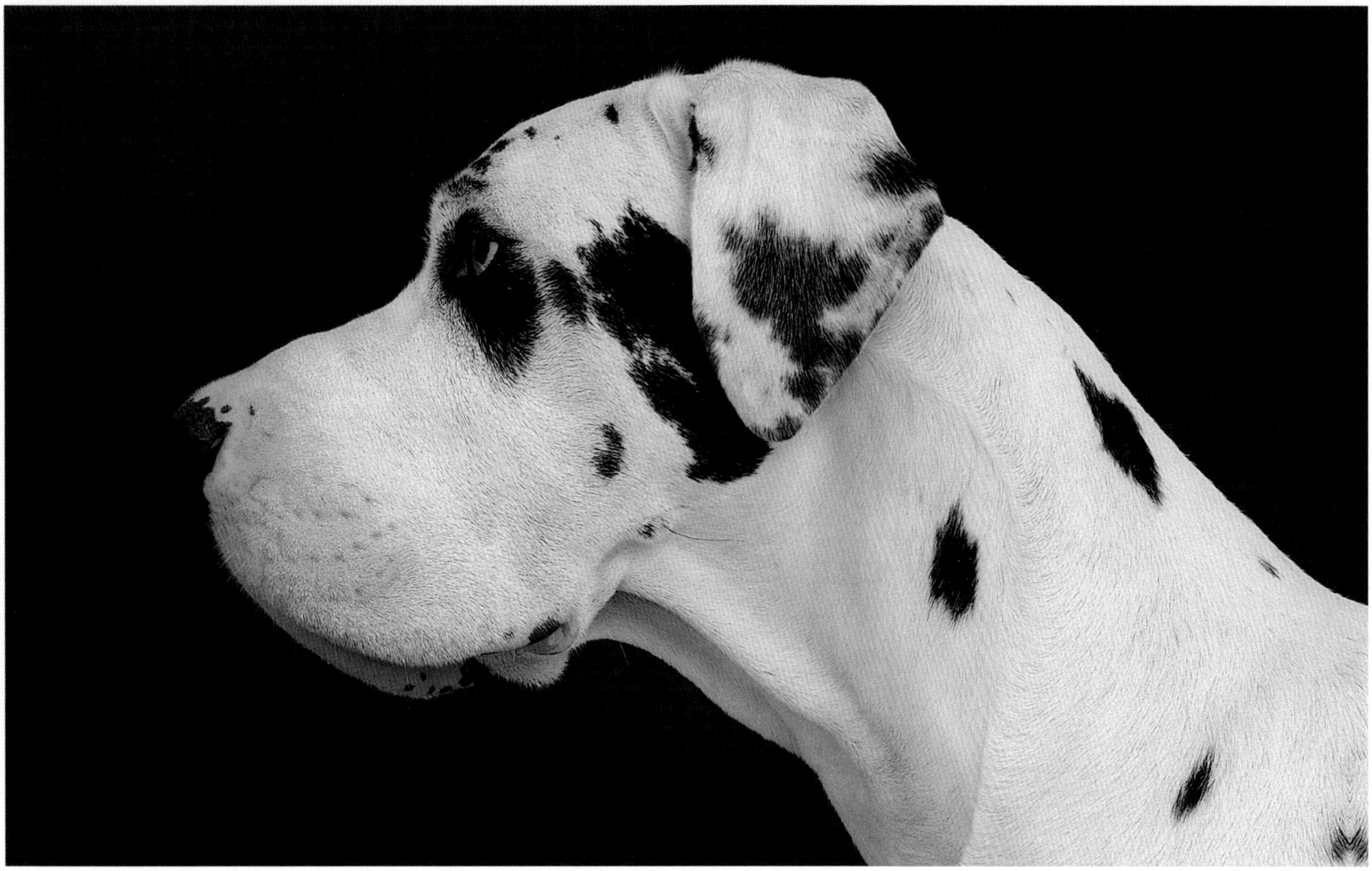

The Hungarian Puli has a unique corded coat shown off to advantage by this grey **(above)** and black masked apricot **(right)**. Originally a herder and drover in its native country, it was first exhibited in Britain around 1950 and has increased in popularity in the last 15 years.

The Newfoundland is another superb water dog which started life as a draught dog in its native Canada. This gentle giant has a natural eagerness to please and an adult male can weigh up to 69kgs (138 lbs). Note the huge paws on this puppy **(right)** and the attractive brown **(opposite)**.

Above: The Norwegian Buhund is a typical spitz breed, with ancient origins in the Icelandic Dog of over 1,000 years ago. Commonly seen in a wheaten jacket **(above)**, they are also acceptable in wolf sable and black coats.

Right and overleaf: The Old English Sheepdog or 'Bobtail' was developed as a working breed in the west country region in the 19th century. It is a profusely coated breed with a wide appeal, but time must be allocated to regular grooming.

Above: Often mistaken for a 'poodle cross' the Portuguese Water Dog is a traditional water breed clipped out over the hindquarters to facilitate swimming in its function of assisting local fishermen to retrieve nets. A keen guard dog, its profuse coat protects it from cold sea temperatures.

Above and right: The Rottweiler, essentially a guarding breed, originates from Rottweil in Germany. It is noted as a loyal working companion and several police forces have used it for patrol work.

Left: The St Bernard was probably brought to Switzerland by the Roman army's northerly push into Europe. In the 1700s references to 'rescue dogs' working out of the Hospice founded by Archdeacon Bernard de Menthon suggest that the use of dogs was an established routine. It is generally accepted that those dogs were finer boned and had less substance than examples of the breed seen today.

Above: An attractive member of the spitz family, the Samoyed originates from Siberia, where it worked as a sled dog, and as a herding and guarding breed. The breed is noted for its melting 'smile', in evidence here!

Left and overleaf: The Shetland Sheepdog is a collie in miniature originally from that northern Scottish isle. A beautiful, intelligent and alert dog, it has a double thick coat, shown to advantage on this sable and white and tricolour.

The Shetland Sheepdogs' mane, frill and feathering are evident in these photos. Note the alert expression and ear carriage **(below)**.

The Siberian Husky originates from north east Asia where it was used as a sledge dog for the Chukshi, a nomadic tribe which inhabited the frozen steppes. The breed boasts a double thick medium length coat to enable it to work in extremely cold climates. The breed is still favoured by sledge enthusiasts today and teams of Huskies regularly compete in timed trials on forest tracks during the winter season.

The Swedish Vallhund only gained formal recognition in the 1940s, and here again is a typical spitz type with cattle herding qualities similar to the Welsh Corgi which must be a distant relative.

The tailed Cardigan Welsh Corgi **(above)** and its close Pembroke cousin **(below and right)** were not recognised as separate breeds until 1934. Essentially a cattle droving breed, they have an appealing foxy expression. The British Royal family also popularised the breed with fine specimens often appearing in family photographs.

TOY GROUP

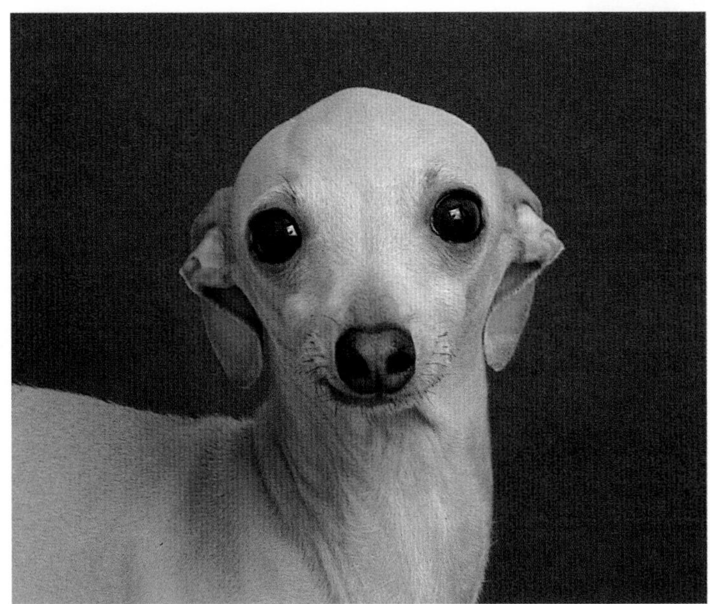

TOY GROUP

As well as their preoccupation with the developments taking place throughout the British Empire, the Victorians also took a keen interest in zoology and stock-keeping, with a particular focus on the Toy Dog group of breeds.

During the Victorian era sporting dog exhibitions and shows extended their classification to reflect "...the increased popularity of these smaller, cosseted dogs particularly favoured by the ladies."

So said Mr Cruft in 1890 when Cruft's own show incorporated Toy Dog Club classes to enhance the show's authority.

Pomeranians were a popular spitz breed in miniature, the Pekingese were greatly favoured by Queen Victoria and Pugs, too, were widespread at that time.

Recent years have seen a sustained increase in Cavalier King Charles Spaniel registrations, whilst the Yorkshire Terrier remains the most popular of the Toy breeds.

Once again the overseas influence on breeds listed within this group is obvious. In a comparatively short period the Bichon Frisé, an appealing white dog of French origin, has attracted wide interest and several breed clubs have emerged to serve these enthusiasts.

The oriental connection via the Pekingese is obvious, but less well known is the Japanese Chin, formerly the Japanese Spaniel.

The Chinese Crested, apart from its crest of hair and tufts on the feet, is a unique hairless dog.

The demands of modern living prevent many people from owning a large dog. Those who don't favour the sporting breeds often turn to this group for a companion or a family pet more suited to their town life.

Nevertheless, the 22 members of the Toy group are truly '*multum in parvo*'.

POINTS TO REMEMBER

This is the smallest group with the smallest dogs, but what variety lies within it!

It is easy to say that these breeds 'lend themselves to modern living,' but close attention has to be paid to these Toys if they are to become part of your life.

Coats range from smooth to profuse, and in terms of character, these dogs range from the aloof to the gay Cavalier which has to be everyone's friend.

A study has indicated that these breeds are more favoured by the elderly and retired, but such statistics are confounded by the emergence of the Yorkshire Terrier and the Cavalier King Charles Spaniel in the top 10 of all breeds over many years.

Remember, despite their smaller appetites and in some cases the need for less exercise, they need every bit as much care and attention as their larger cousins.

The impish Affenpinscher and the Miniature Pinscher were the same breed until in 1896 it was decided to separate the different coated varieties. A game, alert little dog, it is the smallest of all the Pinscher family. The dog on the left with 'prick' ears is a typical German import.

The Bichon Frisé has become a popular breed in recent years but its French origins go back to the 14th century, when Italian merchants were said to have brought these attractive white dogs from the Canary Islands to mainland Europe. The breed was favoured by the royal courts of Europe. and consequently was portrayed in many oil paintings of the time.

The Cavalier King Charles Spaniel is the second most popular of all Toy breeds and its forerunner was the toy spaniel in favour at the time of King Charles II. The variety of colours shown here ranges through the solid ruby (or rich fawn), the blenheim (chestnut and white), black and tan and tricolour. Described as an active, graceful but sparkling character, it is easy to see why it appeals as a family dog.

Above: The black and tan Cavalier has raven black with tan markings above the eyes and on the cheeks, chest and legs.

Above: The whole coloured rich red ruby Cavalier has no white markings.

Above: The tri-colour Cavalier has a well broken black and white coat with tan markings.

Above: The classic popular blenheim Cavalier showing the rich chestnut markings on a predominantly white coat.

The Longcoat Chihuahua **(right)** pictured here and its close cousin the Smoothcoat **(left)** are the world's smallest breeds of dog. The first Chihuahua was registered by the American Kennel Club in 1904. Whilst it is generally accepted that they emanate from the Mexican state after which they were named, they were thought to have arrived there from Pacific trade routes to the far east. Despite their size they have a bold temperament.

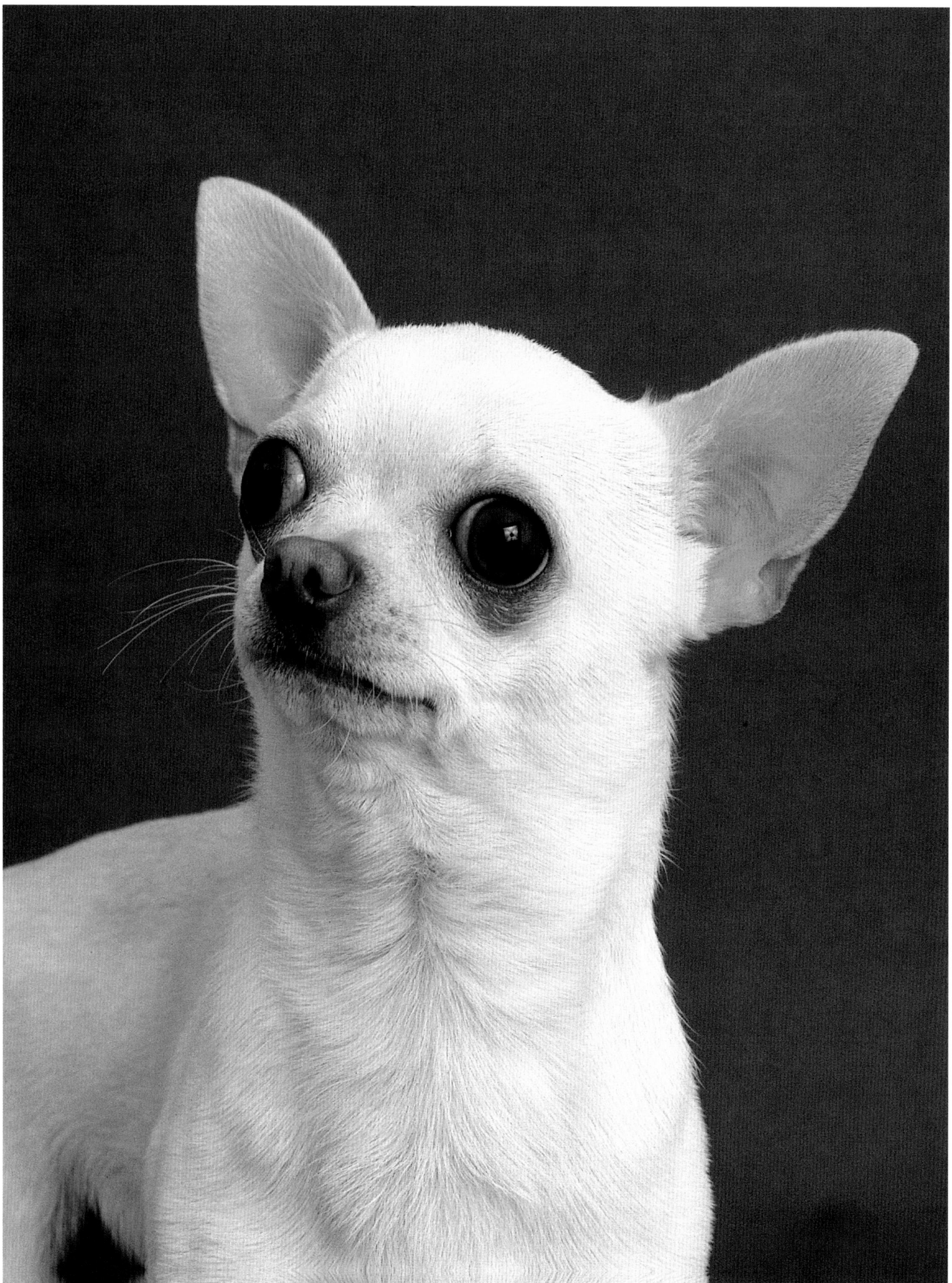

Note the classic 'apple dome' head and large round eyes set well apart on this attractive cream Smoothcoat Chihuahua.

Whilst the origins of the Chinese Crested Dog are obvious, examples of other hairless dogs exist in Africa, Turkey and Mexico.

The featherings on the feet, tail and ears are particularly distinctive. The body skin can be any solid colour or mottled.

Originally known as the Toy Black and Tan Terrier, the English Toy Terrier is essentially a Manchester Terrier in miniature. It gained its reputation in the ratpits of 19th century Britain where its catching technique was tested in competition with other dogs.

The Griffon Bruxellois showing the smooth and rough coated varieties. A native of Belgium, it is an intelligent, well-balanced little dog with an impish, monkey-like expression.

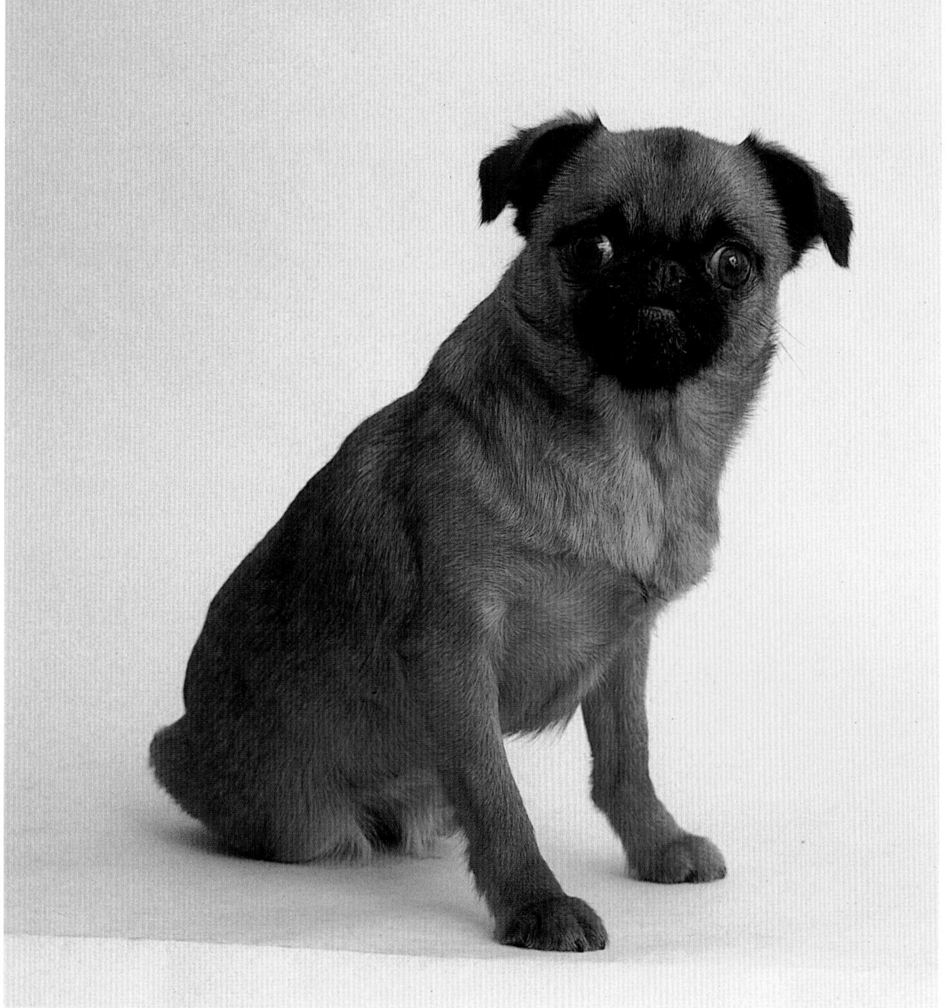

Opposite and left: The Italian Greyhound is a slender and elegant greyhound in miniature. Despite its delicate appearance, it is a fearless character with a gentle, loving nature.

Below and overleaf: The Löwchen is often known as the Little Lion Dog because of the traditional lion clip in which it is presented in the show ring. Its origins are European, probably as a member of the Bichon family, and it has gained popularity over the last 20 years.

The Papillon originated in central Europe evolving as the Dwarf Spaniel in the 16th century. Note the profuse ear fringes and alert expression on these examples of the breed.

The Pekingese was the sacred dog of China, and its history is carefully recorded in carvings, bronzes and paintings going back to the 8th century. The dogs were introduced to Britain in 1860 after the sacking of the Summer Palace in Peking during the Boxer Rebellion. A fawn and white Pekingese is said to have been passed on to Queen Victoria at the time. The fawn with a black mask is the most popular colour but here we also see an appealing black.

Above and preceding page: A black masked fawn Pekingese. Note the broad skull and required profuse coat.

Right and overleaf: As a dainty toy spitz breed, the Pomeranian was a great favourite of Queen Victoria. Its attractive, straight, harsh coat is evident in these orange **(overleaf)** and pale orange **(right)** examples.

The Pug is a native of China and was said to have been brought into Europe by Dutch traders. Clearly defined wrinkles are an important part of the head and expression in this dignified, intelligent dog.

The Yorkshire Terrier is the most popular of all the Toy breeds and overall is rarely out of the top three. A glamorous and fashionable pet in the late 19th century, it attracted large entries at shows, but its origins were modest by comparison. Now considerably miniaturised its predecessors were longer in the leg to enable them to catch vermin. The Yorkshire was thought to have been an amalgam of various sporting Terriers to produce this dog with an attractive silky steel blue coat and tan head markings. Although placed in the Toy group its terrier instinct remains as strong as ever.

INDEX

Affenpinscher 218
Afghan Hound 10, 13, 14, 16
Africa 40, 232
Airedale 92, 95, 96, 119
Akita 127
Alaska 160
Alaskan Malamute 160
America 138
American Kennel Club 228
Arab, Arabian 42
Arctic 184
Asia 207
Australian Cattle Dog 158, 162
Australian Terrier 98

Balmoral 181
Barge Dog (Schipperke) 144
Basenji 16
Basset Fauve de Bretagne 12
Basset Hound 10, 18
Beagle 10, 21
Bearded Collie 164
Bedlington 91, 101
Belgian Shepherd Dog 166, 168
Belgium 236
Bernard de Menthon, Archdeacon 203
Bernese Mountain Dog 171
Bernese Oberland 171
Bichon 239
Bichon Frisé 215, 220
'Bichon type' spaniel 6
Black and Tan Terrier 112
Border Collie 156, 171
Border Terrier 91, 102
Borzoi 22
Bouvier des Flandres 172
Boxer 157, 173
Boxer Rebellion 244
Briard 176
Britain, British 84, 91, 108, 126, 138, 192, 235, 244
British Empire 6
Bull Terrier 92, 102
Bulldog 126, 129, 130
Bullmastiff 179

Cairn Terrier 90, 93, 104
Canada, Canadian 69, 194
Canary Islands 220
Cardigan Welsh Corgi 156, 210
Cavalier King Charles Spaniel 215, 217, 223, 224, 225, 226, 227
China, Chinese 6, 127, 147, 244
Chinese Crested Dog 216, 232
Chow Chow 127, 132
Chukshi 207
Clumber Park estate 78
Clumber Spaniel 51, 78
Cocker Spaniel 50, 78
Count Hamilton 34
Cruft, Charles 6, 214
Crufts Show 6, 22, 90, 119, 120, 214

Dachshund 10, 13
Dalmatian 126, 129, 135
Dandie Dinmont Terrier 26, 90, 107
Deerhound 11
Devon 92
Dobermann Pinscher 182
Dobermann, Louis 182
Dukes of Gordon 61
Duke of Newcastle 78
Dukes of the Weimar Republic 86
Dwarf Spaniel (Papillon) 242

Egypt 6, 16
Elkhound 31
England 45, 91
English Setter 51, 54
English Springer Spaniel 50, 81
English Toy Terrier (Toy Black and Tan Terrier) 235
Eskimo 184
Eskimo Dog 184
Estrela Mountain Dog 184
Europe, European 135, 142, 157, 166, 184, 220, 239, 242, 250

Field Spaniel 51
Finnish Spitz 31, 32
First World War 172, 187
Flatcoated Retriever (Wavy-coated Retriever) 72
Flemish 144
France, French 38, 64, 78, 142, 215
French Bulldog 129

German Shepherd (Alsatian) 157, 187
German Short-haired Pointer 51, 57, 58, 63
German Spitz 127, 129
German Wire-haired Pointer 51, 60
Germany, German 144, 173, 189, 201, 218
Glen of Imaal Terrier 91
Golden Retriever 50, 72
Gordon Setter 51, 61
Grand Basset Griffon Vendéen 12, 40
Grand Duke Nicholas 22
Great Dane 189
Greyhound 11, 13, 35, 45
Griffon Bruxellois 236
Groenendael 168
Guy Mannering (by Sir Walter Scott) 90

Hamiltonstövare (Swedish Foxhound) 34
Harrier 95
Hungarian Puli 192
Hungarian Vizsla 51, 63

Icelandic Dog 196
Ireland 91
Irish Red and White Setter 52
Irish Setter 51, 63
Irish Terrier 91
Irish Water Spaniel 51, 83
Irish Wolfhound 11, 13, 36
Italian Greyhound 239
Italian Spinone 51, 64
Italy, Italian 64, 158, 220

Japan, Japanese 127
Japanese Chin (Japanese Spaniel) 215
Japanese Spitz 127, 135

Keeshond 136
Kennel Club 6, 114, 166, 171
Kerry Blue Terrier 91, 110
King Charles II 223

Labrador Retriever 50, 53, 75, 77
Laekenois 166
Lakeland Terrier 119
Lancashire Heeler 156
Large Munsterlander 69
Lhasa Apso 126, 138, 140, 147
Longcoat Chihuahua 228
Löwchen (Little Lion Dog) 239

Malinois 168
Manchester Terrier 112, 235
Mastiff 158, 179
Mexico, Mexican 228, 232
Miniature Longhaired Dachshund 10, 24
Miniature Pinscher 218
Miniature Poodle 142
Miniature Schnauzer 26, 144
Miniature Smooth-haired Dachshund 10, 27
Miniature Wire-haired Dachshund 26
Montmartre 142

Newfoundland 194
Norfolk Terrier 112
Norwegian Buhund 196
Norwich Terrier 112
Nottinghamshire 78
Novia Scotia Duck Tolling Retriever 69

Old English Sheepdog ('Bobtail') 150, 156, 196

Old English Terrier 95
Otterhound 95

Pacific 228
Papillon 242
Parson Jack Russell Terrier 92, 114
Peking Summer Palace 244
Pekingese 6, 215, 244, 246
Pembroke Welsh Corgi 156, 210
Petit Basset Griffon Vendéen 12, 38
Pharaohs 6, 16
Piedmont 64
Pointer 51, 70
Pomeranian 246
Poodle 126, 129, 142
Portugal 184
Portuguese Water Dog 158, 200
Prince Oldenbourg 22
Pug 215, 250

Queen Victoria 181, 215, 244, 246

Reverend John Russell 92, 114
Rhodesian Ridgeback 11, 40
Rome, Roman 203
Rottweil 201
Rottweiler 201
Rough Collie 157, 181
Russia, Russian 22

Saluki 11, 13, 42
Samoyed 203
Scandinavia, Scandinavian 31, 138
Schipperke (Barge Dog) 144
Schnauzer 6, 144
Scotland, Scottish 61, 91, 104, 107, 116, 156, 164, 171, 181, 205
Scottish Terrier 90, 116
Shar Pei 127
Shetland Sheepdog 157, 205, 206
Shiba Inu 127
Shih Tzu 126, 129, 147
Siberia 203
Siberian Husky 207
Sir Walter Scott 90
Skye Terrier 90
Smooth Fox Terrier 92, 107
Smoothcoat Chihuahua 228, 231
Soft-coated Wheaten Terrier 91
Spitz 31, 203, 215
Spratts 6
St. Bernard 158, 203
Staffordshire Bull Terrier 90, 93, 119
Sussex Spaniel 51, 84
Swedish Foxhound (Hamiltonstövare) 34
Swedish Kennel Klub 34
Swedish Lapphund 158
Swedish Vallhund 158, 209
Switzerland 171, 203

Terveuren 168
The Netherlands, Dutch 250
Tibet, Tibetan 126, 138, 150, 158
Tibetan Spaniel 148
Tibetan Terrier 150
Toy Dog Club 214
Toy Poodle 142
Turkey 232

UK 69, 148, 176
USA 126

Victorian 214

Weimaraner 51, 63, 86
Welsh Corgi 156, 209
Welsh Springer Spaniel 51
Welsh Terrier 119
West Highland White Terrier 90, 93, 120
Whippet 11, 45
Whippet Club 45
Wire Fox Terrier 92, 107, 108

Yorkshire 95
Yorkshire Terrier 215, 217, 252